the **Passionate** *life*

A Blueprint for Achieving Success and Contentment.

the **Passionate** life

A Blueprint for Achieving Success and Contentment.

RAAKESH B. KULWAL

Worldwide Published by
Pendown Press

PENDOWN PRESS

An ISO 9001 & ISO 14001 Certified Co.,

Regd. Office: 2525/193, 1st Floor, Onkar Nagar-A,
Tri Nagar, Delhi-110035
Ph.: 09350849407, 09312235086
E-mail: info@pendownpress.com
Branch Office: 1A/2A, 20, Hari Sadan, Ansari Road,
Daryaganj, New Delhi-110002
Ph.: 011-45794768
Website: PendownPress.com

First Edition: 2023

ISBN: 978-93-5554-524-4

Layout and Cover Designed by Pendown Graphics Team
Printed and Bound in India by Thomson Press India Ltd.

This book is dedicated to all the dreamers, the doers, and the believers. To those who have the courage to follow their hearts and chase their passions, no matter the obstacles in their way. May this book serve as a source of inspiration and guidance as you embark on your own journey to live a passionate life.

Contents

ABOUT THE AUTHOR

The author of 'THE PASSIONATE LIFE' is Raakesh B. Kulwal, a well-known expert in the field of entrepreneurship has dedicated his life to studying and teaching the concepts of passion and purpose, and has inspired countless individuals to live more fulfilling and meaningful lives. With his unique blend of practical advice, personal stories, and powerful insights, Raakesh B Kulwal has created a guidebook that will help readers tap into their own passions and unlock their full potential.

JOURNEY OF THE AUTHOR

Raakesh B. Kulwal is an entrepreneur. He started his career in the jewellery business. At the age of 22, he opened his own jewellery office, however, in 1996, he switched from the jewellery business to the Ghee business in order to assist his father in his family business. Formerly, he worked as a trader and distribution for different companies. Over time, he completely reformed his family business.

As a trader, he evolved into an entrepreneur. Naman, his own brand, is the leading brand in Rajasthan. Today, along with ghee, he has more than 60 different products Well-known people are his prime customers today. He always keeps himself updated with the knowledge to take the business to new heights. Aside from graduating from Rajasthan University, he completed the "Business Coaching India" course and studied business with S.P. Jain in Mumbai. Additionally, he has taken leadership courses at Wharton University He has also attended Tony Robbins' workshops and completed the landmark advanced course and many more.

He loves to read books. He is very fond of music, dance, and interacting with people. His love of reading has helped him develop his creativity and expand his knowledge. Music, dance, and interacting with others have enabled him to learn the value of teamwork and collaboration.

He has a collection of more than 400 books. His main selling point is the generation of original ideas. He has created an era in his family's business. Although, in reaching this point, he has experienced many ups and downs. He rode a wave of success and failure, but he never gave up, keeping his head held high and his dreams fearless. He learned a lot from his experiences and tried to improve every time. He thinks that no one is perfect, but we can make everything perfect by improving ourselves. He also says that success does not come until you fail. Because our failures only serve to highlight our errors and provide us with the opportunity to improve. We must keep trying until we reach our destination.

He is a very sympathetic person. Once he establishes a relationship with someone, he becomes so attached to them that he begins to regard them as family. The employees, family, and friends are all his soul, but he also realises that people, in pursuing their dreams, take their lives, health, and relationships for granted. They do not have time for either of them. Everyone is attempting to cope with one another while losing sight of human values. People have time for social networking but do not have time to spend with their parents, children, or life partners. God has provided all of the means and resources we require to meet our needs, but we still lack time. We know the importance of being healthy, but we still do not focus on our health. We do not have time to exercise or follow a healthy diet. That's why we are not satisfied with our lives. We do not pause to consider where we are heading.

After realising this, a thought came into my mind: What if I could find a way to bridge the gap between our world and the spirit realm, to truly unlock its potential and unlock my own?

To accomplish this, I decided to embark on a spiritual journey of discovery. I should make people aware of this and help them make their lives extraordinary based on what I have learned from my experiences.

This book will take you on a journey through life, where you will recap your life. It will assist you in analysing your life in all aspects: where you are, where you want to go, and where you have arrived. This will also help you realise your drawbacks and find a new way to reach your destination.

Every aspect of your life will be highlighted here. It will help you to make strong relationships in your professional and personal life so that you can live a mentally and physically strong life. It will help you achieve your goals and lead you to a place where you can explore the dynamics of power and authority. In addition, it will challenge your preconceived notions of what it means to be free so you can explore ways to make your life extraordinary.

ACKNOWLEDGEMENT

First and foremost, I would like to express my deepest gratitude to my Guru ji, Shri Guruvanand Swami, and my parents, without whose blessings I was unable to write this book. Their invaluable guidance, direction, and immense love have enabled me to bring out this book. Secondly, I would like to thank my wife, Renu Kulwal, and her friend, Abhilasha, for all the help and support they provided me in completing this book They have made a great effort to shape my ideas into powerful content. They have tried to present all my experiences and lessons in such a way that they can be valuable and life-changing for readers. Then I would like to thank my daughter, Himanshi Kulwal, who has done all the graphics in the book. All the graphics were made after a great deal of thought.

I would also like to thank my editor, for their insights and expertise that helped shape this book into its final form. Their guidance and support have been invaluable, and I am truly grateful for their partnership in this project.

Additionally, I would like to extend my appreciation to the mentors, colleagues, and friends, who have provided me with the knowledge, inspiration, and motivation to pursue my passions and bring this book to life. Your influence has been immeasurable, and I am grateful for all that I have learned from each and every one of you.

Finally, I would like to thank all the readers who have taken the time to pick up this book and explore the ideas within. It is my hope that these pages will inspire and empower you to pursue your own passions and live a life full of purpose and fulfilment.

Thank you for your support, and I hope this book will serve as a helpful guide on your own journey.

Chapter 1

WHAT IS LIFE?

> *"Live the Life of Your Dreams: Be brave enough to live the life of your dreams according to your vision and purpose instead of the expectations and opinions of others."*
>
> **~Roy T. Bennett, The Light in the Heart**

Waking up every day, working out, having breakfast, getting ready, doing daily set tasks, coming home, having dinner, and finally going to bed. Today, when I turn 50, at this significant stage of my life, I can't help but think back on all these years I have spent doing this and wondered, why am I or the people around me following the same routine every day? Are we living happily? Are we satisfied with our lives? What do we think about life? Can we make our life better than what we have today? Can we make it extraordinary?

Life is a priceless, magnificent gift of God. Among all the species, only humans are blessed with emotions, and the ability to think and achieve what they want. We have the power to experiment, learn from our experiences, and produce better results.

Humans are the chosen ones, to have the sensibility to evolve intellectually. We are the only ones who have the power to execute what our minds can think. Life is a journey from birth to death. It is a game of two breaths.

Human beings have evolved from scratch to modern technology. Through so many species, it was only ours that had the sensibility and knowledge to create, innovate and bring our thoughts to living reality.

For us to take birth as humans amongst a million species on the earth, is a blessing from god. When God has blessed us with such a beautiful gift, don't you think it's our responsibility to live our life with a bigger purpose? Each one of us has a role to play in this world. We only get one life. When we set a meaning for our lives, we not only contribute to society, but it also makes life content and more fulfilling for ourselves and our close ones.

When we reach a significant stage of life like I have today, looking back at what you have contributed and achieved should fill you with pride and happiness, not regrets. A lot of us tend to stay in a state of dissatisfaction. Cribbing about how our life is, criticising and blaming others, experiencing jealousy from others' achievements, but continuously making excuses for not putting efforts to improve and change our lives. But we need to accept that our lives are only in our hands and it is our duty to do whatever we can to improve our lives.

We do everyday tasks aimlessly just because we have to. Why are we continuing to follow this routine? Maybe because it works well for us, or is it because we need more time to leave our comfort zone? When we were kids, we had different dreams, but our choices and goals changed as we grew up. Why? Because sometimes destiny has another plan for our life. We decide to go with what life has planned for us by taking a step over our own judgement.

> *Running aimlessly in a rat race doesn't end up being fruitful to anyone. Only when we break out of the loop hole, can we truly achieve something.*

Are we content with this thought? Does it give us satisfaction and happiness from the bottom of our hearts? Can we make our lives better even if the present situation was not a part of our original plan?

While setting out in the world, I learned about the jewellery industry. I was quite young and I was fully convinced and prepared to make the most out of it, however, life had other plans and I had to join my family business. I was not happy with the situation. I couldn't accept that this would be my destiny. But being stuck wouldn't have helped me or my situation. So, I took it positively and started thinking about ways to achieve my dreams. Having walked on this path that was presented to me then, today I have achieved something that surpasses my imagination. I started out as a trader, but today, I am one of the leading entrepreneurs.

Think about how different your life is from what you had thought for it to be. The difference between now and when we were younger is our priorities. When we were young, our motive was to do anything that made us happy. Things that would make us happy and give us peaceful sleep at the end of the day. But as we grow up and take up more responsibilities, we become more practical and start making decisions from various factors like emotions, practicality, and circumstances, and put our happiness on a back burner, like it is not a valid reason. We convince ourselves that we are happy and our life is extraordinary. We make a bubble in our minds to validate our decisions and actions as correct and perfect. We convince ourselves that these decisions are responsible for making our and the lives of our loved ones great. But how true is that? Are you truly happy or are you just settling into your comfort zone?

When we accept the present situation, leaving what we wanted to achieve and being okay with our comfortable life, we limit our happiness. We put a full stop to it. We restrict our growth and level of achievement.

What we don't put a thought to, is life doesn't pause or stop for anyone or anything. Life is all about constantly struggling ahead. You don't get it again or extra time to snooze. Life is about making conscious decisions and moving ahead with them, with a zeal to live. Life is meant to live to its full potential, to move ahead continuously and experience every season, every colour it has to offer. One should always keep moving. We can't take our happiness and contentment for granted. So much so that we don't even consider it something worth working towards.

Life has a lot to give, and it makes it a point to groom and prepare us from time to time for the challenges that await us. God gives us the strength and sensibility to face difficulties. He only presents us with the situations that he thinks we are capable of handling. Then why do we don't keep faith in our dreams and capability to achieve what we have set our mind to?

BREAK DOWN YOUR GOALS INTO SMALL STEPS

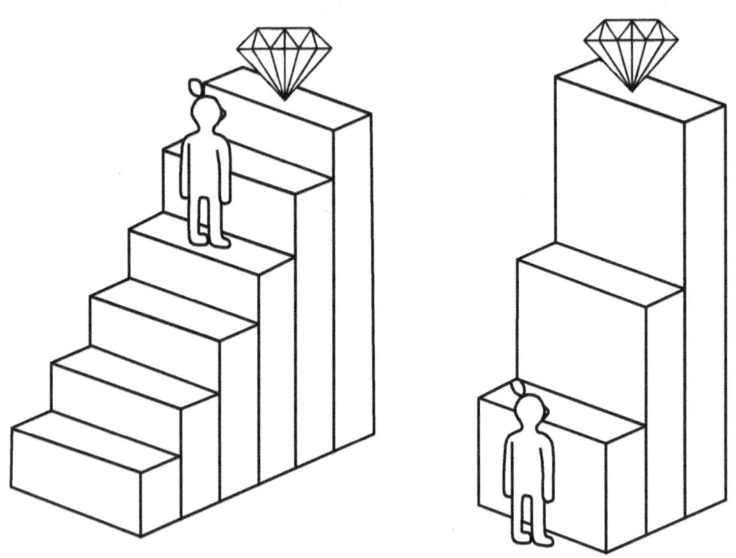

Your dream only seems difficult to achieve when you make it difficult. Every dream is achievable. We just need to take the first step and make the steps gradual and achievable.

We get tired sometimes to the extent that we give up; we don't put effort into changing our circumstances which can improve our future. Not doing something is an action in itself that will not help anyone to succeed in life. Thus, we need to be on our toes, be vigilant and give up our sedentary habits, and be up and about. We need to be aware of ourselves and the need to take charge and keep moving forward for a better and more fulfilling life.

Life is a rainbow full of colours. All of us come across different situations, seasons, emotions, and ups and downs. Our situations make us experience all these colours. Some have us thrilled, some make us feel grateful, some make us sad, and overwhelmed and some situations extend to be such challenges that seem to be never-ending, leaving us feeling even perplexed and confused. Such situations make us question everything and seem nothing less than a nightmare. But, we must learn to embrace life for what it is. We need to keep faith that this too is a phase that shall pass and positive times are ahead of us. As it is said, the brightest sunrise is after the darkest night. But that can only happen if we learn to make the best of our present situation and circumstances through more effort, new ways, faith and, a positive attitude. We should have a strong sense of confidence and we need to trust our instincts to find solutions to move ahead of our present circumstances instead of being stuck in remorse for our failures or misfortunes.

Life is a rainbow full of colors. It is full of
emotions, seasons, circumstances and people.
Life is full of love, laughter, tears and it can all
be experienced to its fullest with us all together!

If we want our life to be extraordinary - we cannot give in to difficult situations. Life is all about continuously fighting for our dreams, building ourselves to make them a reality. Instead of simply accepting defeat and not fighting for what we truly want, can never give us true happiness. When someone gets stuck, gives into stagnation, and stops thinking of moving ahead, it becomes the biggest reason to lead an unhappy and unfulfilled life. How can we stop at one place? How can we stop moving forward? When water gets stagnant in an area, it only gives rise to algae and breeds mosquitoes which can only spread diseases. On the other hand, if that water continues to flow, it keeps cleansing itself and serves as a life resource. Our minds and our lives are the same. If we keep ourselves stuck, it only gives rise to negative circumstances and thoughts of failure but moving ahead and opening our minds gives rise to us discovering new open doors and pathways. But then why do we pretend to be happy and satisfied with what we are doing even when we're not? Because we don't want to leave our comfort zone. We're too comfortable and we know what it looks like if we continue to stay in one profession, one situation, one relationship, etc. We are afraid of the unknown and of learning new things, broadening our thoughts, accepting the changes, and giving a new horizon to our vision. We are so used to our comfort zone, that something stops us from making our life better than what it is today.

Life is a stagnant pond spreading negativity and illness if we stay suck in one place. But it can be as beautiful as heaven if we embrace change, choose positivity and keep moving ahead happily.

This is nothing but fear. Fear of failure. Fear is the biggest challenge and driving force. It may sound intriguing, but it's true. It keeps us from pursuing our dreams, restricts our growth, holds us back, and also stops us from accepting new changes.

But the question is, how do we grow? What will make us grow? For any growth, it is important to ground ourselves first. To progress ahead in the future, first we must concentrate on the present and focus on our lives today.

Today - The Power of The Present

> *"If you want to be happy, do not dwell in the past, do not worry about the future, focus on living fully in the present."*
>
> **~Roy T. Bennett, The Light in the Heart**

Each of us has an ideal picture of our perfect life. That picture shows us exactly what will make us happy, how we want it to be. On the other hand, we also know where we might actually end up given the reality. The distance between our dreams and reality is -action.

For every action, we need a planned way ahead. Whenever we achieve something significant, which generates positivity, growth, or abundance from something essential, it makes us happy. Doing things that we love makes us happy. If we spend even one hour doing something we love, our mind automatically aligns. A lot of clutter gets cleared. We achieve a sense of peace. Our thoughts end up being more streamlined. Why?

Because we dedicate ourselves with complete focus in that one hour to do what we love. If that one hour can impact our minds so much, could we only imagine how peaceful our life can get if we are happy throughout the day? Unfortunately, when we think about that picture-perfect life, we keep procrastinating and postponing our actions, putting it all to some other time or some other day.

To progress ahead and grow further in life, you NEED to pay attention to your present. You NEED to live today, your present movement, to the fullest.

When we were young, we thought we would accomplish everything once we entered college. However, as time passed, we further delayed our plans until we started working. After securing a good job, we continued to postpone our goals even further, and this cycle repeated itself after getting married. Eventually, we reach a point where we no longer have the opportunity, time, or physical health to make positive changes in our lives.

A very significant role in our life is of the present moment. Today. Right Now. For people living close to the poles, the night lasts for months and so does the day. They are not fortunate enough to see the brightness of the sun every day or experience the harmony of night every day. Similarly, we don't know what our life has in store for us in the next moment, so why do we delay taking the actions we want to right now? Whatever we want to achieve, whatever we want to do, we must do it today. The right time is here and it is now.

Take a step back and review your life from a broader perspective. Ask yourself, where do you want to see yourself when you are at the age of 70? Also, where will you be at the age of 70 if you continue to live your life the way you live it today? Try to identify the gap between the two. How different are these realities from each other? It is this gap that keeps us from living the life that we want to. Life is a game of choices we make at every moment. Taking responsibility for each decision and situation gives birth to a consciousness that enables us to strive for a better life.

Taking responsibility means taking action which is thought through and aligned with what we want. Today, the time which has passed is the life we already have experienced. The next moment is the most unreliable and uncertain entity. We may or may not even have it. Our only control is over our minds, thoughts, and actions in the present moment. Life is now. It is the moment in which we are living. The day we start living with this reality as the ultimate truth, our attitude will transform. Instead of procrastinating, we will start doing things that greatly benefit us. We would cherish each moment as if it were our last. Then why are we holding ourselves back? Why do we succumb to the fear of failure instead of being fuelled by the fear of being stuck?

Life is a progressive chain. It doesn't function in simultaneous clusters but follows a linear path. We can tread ahead step by step. Each day is new; each moment is an opportunity for us to utilise. Each drop makes an ocean, each moment makes a day, and each day makes our life. It is essential for us to realise that to achieve our desired life at 70; we must start right now. We need to choose to build the life that we want, and we need to start now.

We can lay the foundation of the future only by learning from our past mistakes and working in the present. Only by considering the Past, Present, and Future together, can we make our life better and achieve our dreams.

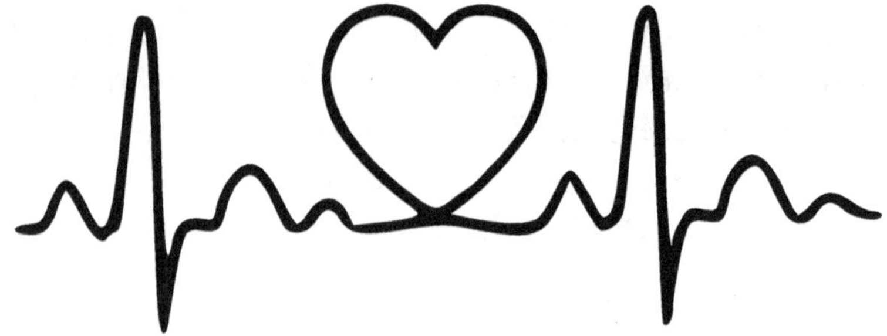

Life is a mix of ups and downs.

Life is only lived when the ecg graph moves up and down continuously, in an uneven rhythm. If the graph is calm and still, just a line, it is no longer a life.

When I got into my family business of ghee distribution, I made it my life's aim to become "Ghee King" and since the day I stepped into the business, I had made it a point to do whatever it takes to be that and continue to do so. I continue to seek new ways of innovation, growth not only for the business but for myself too. I participate in various workshops and continue to learn to increase my knowledge, strength, and capability. Expanding my business and accepting the changes I came across in life, I learned from my circumstances, mistakes and many curve balls that life had to throw in my path but I still continue to improve and grow, but I refuse to stop.

> *Life is not what will happen tomorrow, it is not what happened yesterday, it is what is happening in this moment right now.*

Yesterday has already passed, if you have today, it is a gift and opportunity from god for you to continue. Uncertainty is the beauty of the future because it is so fluid that it can only be moulded through our actions today. God has left the beauty and the picture of our future to be made in our own hands.

It is up to us how beautiful we want to make it. Today is neither concerned with your past nor worried about the uncertainty of the future; it is a free and valuable opportunity in and of itself. So, let go of the past, hold a vision of your future in your heart, and take action with determination to make your life more beautiful and extraordinary.

GRATITUDE – APPRECIATING SELF AND ALL THAT IS GOOD

> *"Let us rise up and be thankful, for if we didn't learn a lot today, at least we learned a little, and if we didn't learn a little, at least we didn't get sick, and if we got sick, at least we didn't die; so, let us all be thankful."*
>
> **~Buddha**

When life throws very challenging obstacles toward us and we feel there is no way to move ahead, we feel like we have failed. It is quite challenging to have a positive outlook and look for a way out. In such a situation of complete darkness, counting the positives we have, shines like a beacon of light. Counting our blessings, and being thankful for the things which are still stable, which provide us comfort, and help us survive is the first and most important step to gaining the power to keep us moving ahead, no matter how challenging our situation may be.

In the most trying and testing situations, what gives us strength? Our physical health supports us to do the hard work we need to do to get closer to our goals. It is our mental health that helps us to be present for our loved ones in their time of need. When we are in a situation to choose a better of two difficult paths, it is our loved ones and elders who are there for us to provide us with their wisdom.

> *Whenever we are in a dilemma, it is the gratitude for the most basic things that uplifts us and shines as a beacon of light in dark times.*

Even after a challenging day at work, it is the comforting home-cooked meal and our bed that gives us relaxation and calms us down. In a testing situation that you may not be able to handle just by yourself, it is your friends and family who come to help you. Having the comfort of home, shelter over our heads, meals to fill us, support of our close ones, and the means and resources to provide support in difficult times have become such basic things for so many of us, that we take them for granted and don't even consider them to be worth being thankful for.

When we start looking at our life on a daily basis, we realise we have so much that makes us who we are. We slowly become more aware of so much that we have, it humbles us and helps us analyse our lives and ultimately ourselves. This starts from within. Making self-introspection and offering gratitude for the positives of life a habit gives us the answers we seek and keeps us grounded.

When we consciously take out a few minutes every day to acknowledge and be thankful for everything we have and all the positivity in our life, it will keep us more aware of the true reality of our life. Making this a habit will not only keep us humble at our best but also will give us the strength we need at our worst.

We can only identify the things which are important to us by knowing ourselves, and self-introspection helps in exactly that. We must spend time with ourselves and make introspection a habit. It is not a task we do once in a blue moon. It's a habit, a lifestyle, a continuous process that builds stronger with each day. It opens the gateway to a better life.

By analysing and evaluating, we can quickly and easily pinpoint our thoughts, and actions and identify our mistakes. This helps us to improve and make our life better. This also helps us continuously know the people and things we have by our side. This helps us build a strong faith in the positives and support systems in our life which leads to a grounded and more aware thought process.

Think of it as getting to know someone and developing a new relationship. To make our life extraordinary, we need to broaden our perspective. We have to think more objectively and rationally. We have to overcome our fear and have to accept the changes. This will help us to take a step out of our present situation and look at the big picture of our life.

1. Go back and think about how limitless you were as a child or a young adult. List the dreams you had as a child that you gave up on due to circumstances and challenges.

1.

2.

3.

4.

5.

6.

7.

2. List the things from above that you can still resume or incorporate into your life. Also mention how you can continue to make them a part of your life.

1.

2.

3.

4.

5.

6.

7.

3. List the things for which you are grateful

1.

2.

3.

4.

5.

6.

7.

4. List the habits you want to get rid of to be more positive and aligned in your life

1.

2.

3.

4.

5.

6.

7.

5. If you knew that today was your last day. list the things below that you would stop postponing and do immediately.

1.

2.

3.

4.

5.

6.

7.

Chapter 2

MINDSET AND WANTS
THE ULTIMATE GOAL

> *"Happiness depends on your mindset and attitude."*
>
> **~ Roy T. Bennett, The Light in the Heart**

Our childhood and how we grew up significantly affect how we become as humans. Children have minds like clay. They get moulded as directed by the circumstances and people around them. What they see and how they are treated plays a major role in their personality development. It makes them more flexible or rigid. More kind-hearted or more self-centred. How a person is brought up ultimately shapes the kind of human they become. When kids observe the patterns or deeds around them, they quickly pick them, and it becomes a part of their behaviour. This paves the path to building the emotional understanding they take with them through life.

How we react to situations reflects the patterns of emotional comfort and openness we have experienced throughout life. One may have tears in their eyes even at the slightest happy moment, while someone may find it almost impossible to cry in the most devastating situation.

Our childhood shapes how we become as adults, if we have lived in a loving, positive and accepting environment, our mindset and values are sure to reflect the same.

When we form strong connections and relationships, our decisions don't remain limited to just ourselves. In very close and strong relationships, our choices also impact the lives of those connected to us. Human beings are social animals. We survive and grow through co-existing and co-creating. We are the most vital resources and support systems for each other. This mutual connection with each other and the things we create is what gives rise to our emotions.

Emotions end up grasping our minds very firmly. We tend to get triggered, affected, and uplifted through actions or circumstances that strongly affect anything we care about. Why?

Because the emotions and expectations of people close to us also get involved. As we grow up and get more exposure through our friends, community members, and surrounding influences, we learn about more ways of living, different mindsets, and methods of attachment and connections. We get exposed to other things that better suit our lives and relationships. This allows us to evaluate our emotional patterns, passion, thinking, feelings, and mindset. We learn that transforming ourselves is a significant need in constantly developing our behaviours and interactions. It is a conscious choice to adapt. This is the key to growing continuously in life if we choose to have an open mind toward diversity and change. The two significant aspects that play a crucial role in keeping this understanding are our mindset and values.

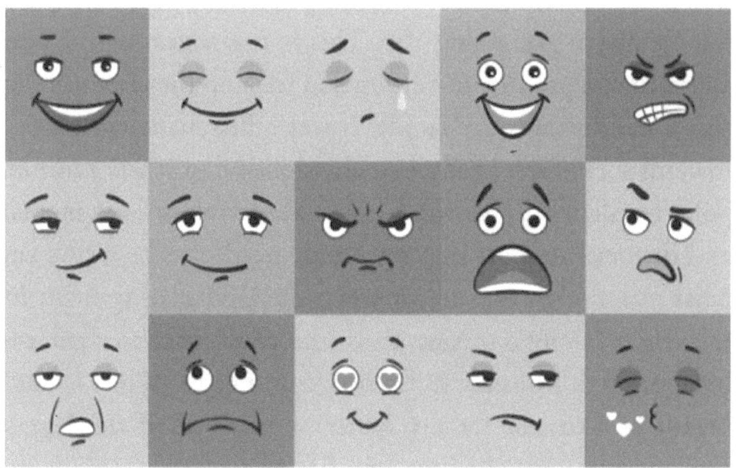

Emotions are a part of the core of a human being. It is astonishing to see not only how one person can feel so many of them at once but also the degrees in which they affect us!

I had always wanted to become a jeweller. It was my dream and I inaugurated my office with a lot of enthusiasm, happiness, and joy. However, when circumstances became difficult and testing, I had to make a choice. Being the only son, the responsibility of continuing the legacy of my family business came onto my shoulders. My family has always been a priority for me above everything else. This is the reason why I went ahead to compromise my dream and took up the responsibility that I had towards my family. It was a life-changing decision towards something I had never envisioned, but it was a turning point for all of us. This one decision was the emotional, mental, and financial support that my family needed to be secure and be at peace. This one decision became a pillar of strength for the entire family and gave them the confidence to fight and breakthrough from the difficult circumstances. While it was a breath of fresh air for my father, it was one of the biggest challenges for me. For me, my life had taken a 180-degree turn. What I had envisioned, learned, dreamt, and strategize to build, was the complete opposite of the traditional family business which I had never intended to pursue.

Taking such big decisions can be extremely challenging and life-changing. Not only for you but also for the people closely attached to you. Such decisions often need us to compromise on various factors to keep things stable emotionally, mentally, and financially.

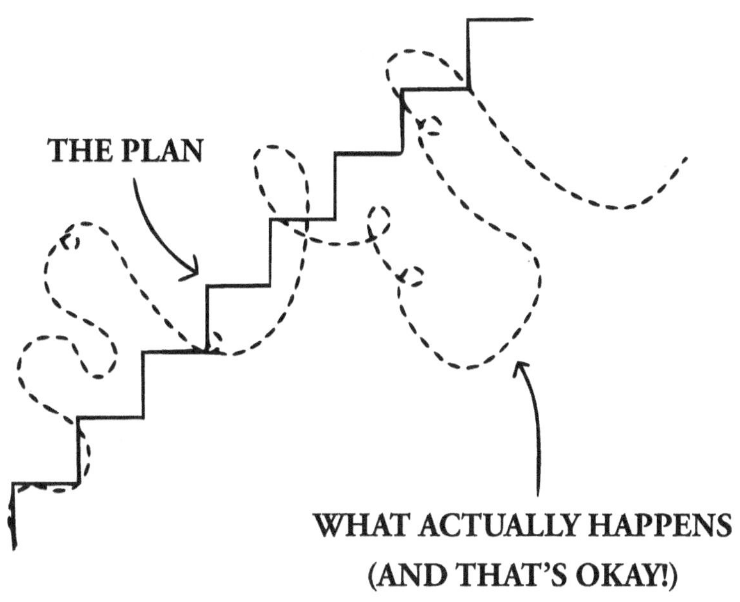

Life never goes according to a set plan, sometimes it changes its course, sometimes we choose to steer it elsewhere, but that IS life! And that IS the fun!

Not just for a short period but many years until you can achieve that stability again. But if you see, in the longer run, this change was necessary. You can only make people around you happy if you are comfortable and satisfied. Making this change may be a challenge for short periods, but it will lead to a happier life with no regrets or remorse.

Change is the turning point and a key factor in life. Everything in our surroundings evolves. The moon is different each night, the weather is different each day, and nature keeps changing constantly. Over the years, everything even in the material world changes, our lifestyle, our relationships, lifestyle change, but it is our thought process that needs to evolve with everything else also. We become so comfortable in the ways of our being, that change feels extremely challenging for us. We are afraid to accept that change is a must for growth to make a better life. Change is the only constant. It doesn't apply only to the changes that happen to us but also to the changes we need to bring to adapt to situations or build the life we want. We don't take big decisions in life because we are afraid. We become scared of its impact on our lives and those attached to us. We become scared of the reaction of our loved ones toward our decisions. Will they be able to accept it happily? Will this decision lead to a happy and successful life? Will it make me and the people connected to me happy?

"Embarking on major life changes is no less than taking a big leap of faith. Instead of being afraid of the gap, think about how amazing it will be on the other cliff!

When we attach so many factors to our choices in life, it becomes easier not to go forward and bring a change.

The most important and primary thing is to overcome our fear of change. This fear keeps us from actually exploring the possibilities our life has to offer. When we are able to do that, we automatically gain a space of acceptance in our minds. This acceptance gives us the threshold to experiment and do something new and make new beginnings in life. No matter what the outcome is, we can only see it once we take the leap. We can only get to know about the outcomes once we simply try. The outcome can be negative or positive. If it ends up being positive, it gives us a boost and propels us forward in the direction with a lot of positivity and energy. But what happens in the other situation? When we are faced with a negative outcome, we end up losing hope and keep doubting and questioning ourselves. This makes us reserved in taking a bold step in the future and doesn't consider making changes to be significant.

In such a situation, we need to remember one thing, change is not just about only moving forward, it is a journey that makes us resilient and helps us to know and test our potential. Situations or circumstances do not determine the outcome of our actions, but our mindset does. Success or happiness depends on our perspective on our situation and what we make of it. Our behaviour, attitude, and thought process don't only depend on how we are brought up but also on our environment. If we are surrounded by people who always talk about progress, who are happy in every situation, and who talk about the solutions instead of being pessimistic, critical, or disappointed, our thought process will evolve in the same direction. Our perception of life will become similar.

Our mind space is like a personal garden that we need to continuously water and tend to. If the mindset is the climate, then the state of mind is the weather. It can change quickly and is never constant. It affects how we interact with people, how we deal with people, how we treat our relationships, how we handle our work and everything in our daily life. The way each moment forms a day and ultimately forms ours. Each reaction creates our interactions, eventually including the life we build for ourselves. Our mind is the director of the way our life takes turns. This is why we need to be aware and particular about the state of mind we function from and each of our actions and reactions. When a drop falls on a large still water surface, it disturbs the stillness of the entire water body; the action causes a similar ripple effect on ourselves and others and hence creates a situation that becomes a part of our lives.

You will notice that whenever we are in an uplifted mood, we encounter problems with a calm mind, irrespective of their magnitude, and start seeking solutions.

> *There is both, negative and positive in all of us.*
> *The direction that our life takes, depends solely*
> *on which one we want to take advice from.*

We prepare ourselves to move mountains and swim seas to make ways out and carve our paths. Our mind reminds us of that one ray of light that breaks the darkness of a dark knight at dawn, giving a way to a bright sunny day. In a positive state of mind, we try to drive each situation toward a positive outcome. Our attitude is more giving, more generous, and more open in our relationships. Growth, positivity, and prosperity stem from such a state of mind and make our surroundings and life beautiful. In a positive state of mind, we make decisions that will make us happy. We accept challenges with the zeal to conquer. It makes us feel substantially accomplished and satisfied. When we know the meaning of satisfaction for us, we know what makes us happy. In a positive state of mind, we drive each situation toward a positive outcome.

On the other hand, when we are low, we feel depressed and nothing seems to cheer us up. We will see everything from a negative perspective, unable to find the solutions even if the answers might be right in front of us. We sometimes also tend to get afraid of being happy, thinking that there is surely something negative waiting for us on the other side. Because of such a mindset, we are unable to embrace happiness with open arms. We end up in a loop of self-doubt and start believing that our efforts will not yield any fruits.

A Zen state of mind, or a stable state of mind, is a neutral zone. It is open and regular. It can process changes and have patience; even in adverse situations, it seeks to exercise patience and knows that this, too, is a phase. A negative state of mind gives way to feelings of anxiety and instability; we become unsatisfied with our life and constantly concentrate on the lack of our life. This gives rise to a lack of trust that anything good will happen. In the presence of negativity, faith can never reside. In such a state, we find it difficult to trust people. A negative state of mind causes us to be stuck in the current situation. Our thought process doesn't expand, limiting our focus to the problem at hand and an immediate solution. We cannot think about the repercussions of that quick solution in the long run because our brains cannot believe that far. So instead of focusing on happiness, our focus is limited to instant problems and solutions.

We cannot achieve greatness with a small mind. We cannot achieve happiness with a lack of energy. The people who are successful and happy in life are the ones who have focused on making decisions that will result in positive things in their life. They focus on achieving and just achieving. There will be failures or lows along the way, but they deal with them to rise again. Life is beautiful. The lows make us appreciate and value the great times, while the highs motivate us to aim higher and keep moving upwards. This state of mind is what multiplies in our lives.

It is all about channelizing our negative thoughts into positive thoughts and actions. The minute we choose to switch and channel, we will see the change in our lives.

Both these states of mind are a spiral. If we are not conscious of choosing our actions and making our decisions, we get caught in either of the waves and our lives shape like that. When we have a negative mind, we remain stuck just looking at the immediate future. The sad part is that most of us are stuck in this dangerous loophole. We don't take a moment to stop and evaluate our lives at a broader level. We don't even consider the results of our actions or reactions.

Like a ripple effect, when we interact, our state of mind dramatically impacts the other person's state of mind. We all communicate with our house helpers or security guards at different places but don't even acknowledge their presence. Instead, when they are not working up to our expectations, it is a reflex action for most of us to shout at them or to criticise them unpleasantly. Try greeting your house help or watchman with a smile as an experiment. Ask them how they are and if they're doing well and see the difference. It is a real example of approaching things with a positive state of mind. That one positive gesture would uplift their mood and, in return, yours. Automatically, you'll also see the difference in how they work for you and even how you communicate with them. A small gesture from a positive state of mind boosts the entire situation. It goes a long way in how we share and becomes a habit. And habit becomes the character.

Similarly, in a negative state of mind, if you ignore them or just keep criticising them, they will feel demotivated. It wouldn't improve their work or duty towards you, but they will loathe you. This situation has become a harmful crisis with just an essential habit change. A positive state of mind is a way of living. It is a lifestyle. The day we take responsibility for our actions, words, and decisions, we can change our lives. Actions and words are like bullets. Once they're shot, they cannot be taken back. This is all the more reason we should be careful from the root. What we think, what we speak, what we do, and ultimately, where we take our lives. A positive state of mind needs constant evaluation and upgrade. It is a conscious choice that we make every day. When we start to achieve, it feels good and positive. This gives rise to the want to achieve more and more. This is the road to success. Every successful person in the world knows what their ultimate goal is. Every happy person knew what made them happy and made conscious efforts. We seek motivation and inspiration when we know what we want to achieve. We look at the people who have achieved what we desire. We try to learn from their journey, their decisions, and their life. Why? No two trips are the same; no two circumstances are the same. But, when we see that someone has achieved what we desire and look at their journey, our faith in our goals grows stronger. They become attainable and tangible for us. It shows us that our goals are achievable and not just a thought. When we get this push forward, it becomes just about our efforts, how we continue to work ahead, and us ultimately achieving our goal.

The fundamental truth is a positive state of mind and is essential. Each small positive action, situation or act of happiness results in enormous positivity and positive results. As small as eating your favourite ice cream on a summer evening or having a cup of chai on a monsoon evening, it helps you to be content. It helps your mind to feel happy and at home. Each small act can make our life happy; we need to grab it as it will give rise to more positive decisions in our lives, even in the most crucial situations.

It is not always possible to continuously be in a peak positive state of mind through everything, but it is vital to strive to come back to a stable state of mind. When situations get tough, when life happens, and things may be out of control for us, we must be conscious about not staying in a negative state of mind. Can we switch from a negative to a positive state of mind immediately? Probably not. But it is essential to at least come to a stable mind. Only through clarity of mind will we be able to think clearly. Make excellent and rational decisions and be able to face different life situations well. Our mind is not only the part we can control consciously but also a part of our mind that we have no direct control over. It is our unconscious mind. Our state of mind and energy significantly impact the thoughts that formulate in the background of which we are unaware.

As said before, change is the only constant in this world. Often, changes are out of our hands. We are afraid of the unknown. Hence we get scared and unbalanced whenever a change comes our way which is out of our control. When that creates a disturbance, it is uncomfortable for us. We get so used to our comfort zone, that accepting any new and unpredictable change is challenging. In such a situation, most of us resort to a negative state of mind in the blink of an eye instead of evaluating the problem with a zen state of mind. Being the most significant challenge we need to conquer, fear of change, fear of the unknown, and fear of uncertainty gets the better of us. We need to learn how to use this fear. Since it is a prominent driving force, it is also a significant reason for giving direction to us in life. Adverse outcomes of the past and fear of not achieving what we truly desire to limit us from taking the leap of faith towards our wants or bringing a change in our lives. We continuously doubt the outcome and our ability to achieve it.

In such a negative state of mind, it becomes difficult for us to think positively. How do we change the spiral, then? The trick is as simple as lessons of the past. Are we resorting to a stable state of mind and thinking about why we were not able to achieve something similar in the past?

What we are from within is what we spread around ourselves. If we choose to stay positive, our aura becomes positive and everything around us, too, reflect the same energy.

What patterns or methods do we need to change to achieve what we want? Is there anything I have developed or need to develop to achieve what I desire? With this slight shift, you will notice that your attitude towards the problem changes. It becomes more solution-oriented. It was as simple as shifting perspective and shifting from a negative thought process to a stable one, which may turn into a positive state of mind.

The kind of mind we have, the similar energies we will exude around us. Often, we talk about the aura of a person. You must've felt very positive and at ease in the presence of someone, while you may feel highly uncomfortable in the surroundings of someone else. What is this aura? Aura is nothing but the energy we spread out in the world. This energy stems from our minds, interactions with people, and actions. Successful people have potent auras. Instantly you feel accountable to them. You feel energised to the point where no task seems difficult to be achieved. When you meet a person who is always in a negative space and stuck to the limitations, you focus on all the negatives of your life. How? This is nothing but a play of energy. Auras can be positive and negative. The power we spread or come into contact with becomes a significant force behind our actions, words, and decisions.

Both these positive and negative states of mind are endless spirals. Once we adapt to either of them, we get sucked into that way of living. Not only do our decisions stem from similar energy, but we attract situations and realities in our life of that very energy. We also affect the people around us and their state of mind through ours. Our aura becomes what we think.

Its strength also becomes stronger or weaker according to the power of our beliefs.

Living through a positive state of mind is a practice. We get better with each situation and each thought. But we do need to realise for us to make this a good practice, for a good life, our values, goals, priorities and direction in which we need to take our life needs to be aligned.

Your core is more important than anything you have been or you will ever be. It is extremely important to know yourself and your core values, mindset, emotions and the state of mind from which you function.

1. List down 5 positive emotions you feel often and how you react to them usually.

Emotion	Reaction

2. List down 5 negative emotions you feel often

Emotion	Reaction

3. What are Your Trigger Points For:

    a. Your Positive Emotions

    b. Your Negative Emotions

4. Now, look back at the above emotional reactions, and list what you think will be a more healthy reaction that you need to practise to achieve a Zen state of mind in a triggered situation.

Emotion	Current Reaction	Desired Reaction

Chapter 3

FEAR

> *"Too many of us are not living our dreams, because we are living our fears."*
>
> **~Les Brown**

In the previous chapter, we learned that success or happiness all depends on how we see life. We all want happiness, prosperity, and growth, but somewhere we are reluctant to accept and bring changes. Why? What is stopping us from finding the will to bring about necessary changes in our life? FEAR. It is a big force that becomes an obstacle in the path of us achieving success.

In our childhood, we were not afraid of anything or anyone. We just played fearlessly and with the ultimate zest. Even if we fell, we got back up and continued. We would never pay attention to the injury, instead, our playtime held more value for us. However, as we grew up, and got attached to multiple factors, a sense of fear stays in our hearts. We are afraid of taking risky decisions due to the fear of losing. As we grow, we become more experienced and mature enough to make correct decisions, but unfortunately, more often than not, our mind gets clouded with this fear. We are unable to gather enough courage to take action for a better life.

GREATEST FEAR
of each enneagram type

All of us have different kinds of fears, It is not something successful people don't have. But, once you are able to identify YOUR fear, it gets easier to fight and move past it towards a better life.

Sometimes, we tend to also over think our circumstances and create a cloud of various outcomes. In our heads, we keep creating scenarios that are not even there. We think about all the negative outcomes that there can be and succumb to their fear. Our hands freeze and we are unable to take any action forward.

Fear can have various forms:

- Fear of losing - resources, relationships, happiness, etc.

- Fear of failure - not being successful in a lifelong dream.

- Fear of achieving great heights - of being unable to handle what we desire if we get it

- Fear of trying something new - if it is not successful, wastes our time

- Fear of change - the cost we might have to pay in case the path we take may not be as fruitful

- Fear dominates our life so much that we lose all our confidence.

We fuel our fear with so much power, that we become unsure even about our correct decisions. We beat ourselves down so much that we lack the confidence to get up and learn something new. Instead of doing something to make our life better, and happier, we limit ourselves because of fear and wait for some miracle to happen that can bring ultimate happiness.

> *"Fear cuts deeper than swords."*
> **~George R.R. Martin, A Game of Thrones**

Fear makes us weak; it swallows our confidence. Fear is the fog on our windscreen. It fogs and disables us to see the path forward. When we try to do something new, our mind gets clouded with a thousand questions and negative outcomes. We tend to get scared and fear cripples us, freezing. Will I be able to do it? Is this the correct decision? What will society say? What will happen if I fail? Will I be judged for my choices?

All these questions give birth to over thinking and fear. At this point, it is difficult to find enough courage to make the right choices. Fear keeps us from reaching the next level of success or fulfilment. When we start to give in to negative thoughts and negative outcomes, our mind starts believing that it is the only way forward. Our mind starts to believe that no good is possible for us, no positive outcomes are possible for us, and we begin to doubt ourselves greatly. All of us have an element of fear in us. How is it that some people are actually able to achieve what they really wanted to in life? Why 90% of the world's wealth is owned by only ⅓ people? Are they fearless? No, all of us have the element of fear in us. But, they chose and realised that what they wanted was more important than their fear.

REACHING YOUR GOAL

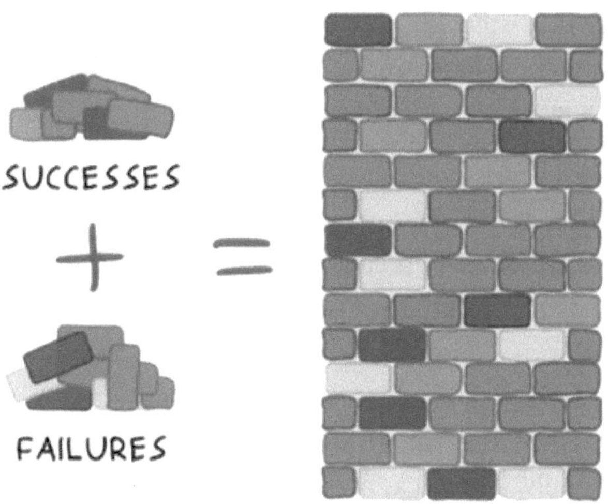

> *Success is not about consecutive right decisions, but it is about the important right decisions you took after learning through the failures of the wrong ones.*

They did not lose hope and confidence because they did not allow their fear to dominate their life. Successful people are not those who got everything right in the first go, but the ones who may have failed many times and faced many critical problems in life. The point always was that they converted their weaknesses into their strengths. Their focus was only on their goals. Although successful people know that the world is continuously watching them, that doesn't affect them and they do what they intend to do.

When I was younger, I was fearless. I always did what I wanted to do. When I started my business, I achieved a lot of success. I never bothered much about what society, people, or friends had to say because I was confident about whatever I did. But as I moved ahead and grew, I started to become more cautious about my choices and decisions. At a lot of points, I had the fear of losing or have been very protective of my family. I would know in my heart that the path I wanted to choose to embark upon was correct for me, but something still kept me stuck. When my elder daughter showed her wish to go abroad for further studies. I disagreed, although I wanted her to go ahead and flourish, I did not have the courage to let her go.

Why? Was I overprotective about my daughter? I was not happy with the decision of letting her go, but because I knew deep in my heart that it is for her betterment, I began trying to overcome my fear of letting her go. I tried to realise that being overprotective of my daughter will limit her potential. Today, I feel proud because she is my strength in my business, being a strong shoulder of support. Once you overcome your fear, after the first most challenging step, moving ahead on the path becomes easier. While I was scared the first time I was faced with this situation with my elder daughter, I became more certain and confident to send my other two kids abroad. Similarly, I continue to try to overcome my life fears. I have realised that anxiety does not help anyone, it makes you weak. One mantra, that has changed my life is-

> *'Nothing is impossible.'*
> *For me it is, I M possible.*

We need to take fear as a positive push. Failures are only the way to success. But putting a stop to your life because of fear is not the way to progress. Self-doubt, and uncertainties lead us to fear. Do you realise the things you are losing because of fear?

- Success
- Happiness
- Confidence
- Peace of mind

SUCCESS

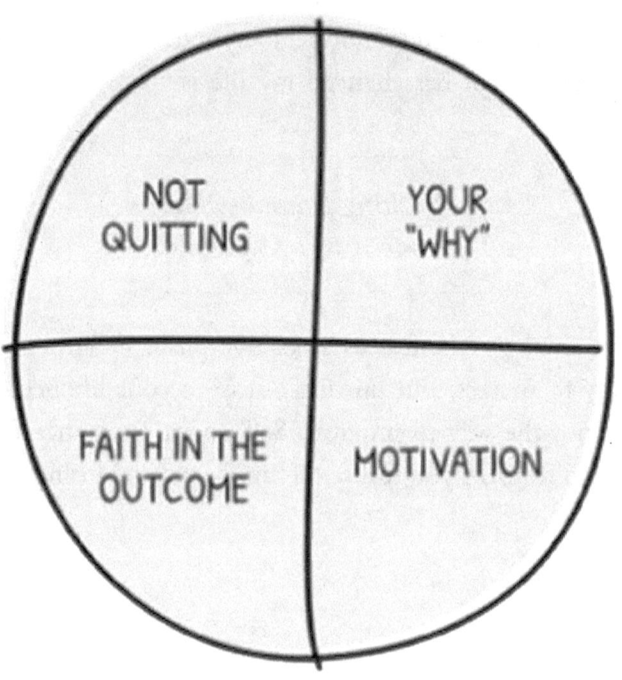

Keeping yourself motivated, not quitting, knowing your reason for making the efforts and having faith in the outcomes are the guiding lines which form a wheel for you to help move past your fear, towards success.

Fear does not allow you to step out of your comfort zone. We need to confront our fear. We cannot stop in our life just because of fear. If we give into fear, not only are we letting ourselves down, but also our close ones. How can you evolve or develop if you give in to your fear? How will you achieve success in your life? How will you make your and others' lives extraordinary?

> *"Do one thing every day that scares you."*
>
> **~Eleanor Roosevelt**

When we achieve success after facing various ups and downs, we feel a sense of achievement and pride. We feel renewed and energised. We realise that, yes, we can do this. We can overcome our fear only by taking action. We should keep on trying unless we achieve success. We have to believe that we can do it, and dare to move forward despite the fear. Make your weakness your strength. All the opportunities will present themselves to you. Instead of dwelling and over thinking about the result; just go ahead and take action with a positive attitude. The only way to deal with your fear is by using the three Fs.

- Face it,

- Fight it,

- Finish it.

What we need to do is face our fear. It is necessary to gain power over your fear. You can only do that by facing it and building the courage to do something about it. Once you do that, you must fight it. It can be a little overwhelming at first, but you'll see that an uncomfortable situation is only for a very short time period as compared to the satisfaction and relief you get for the rest of your life. If you have stage fright and you need to get up on the stage and address a thousand people, of course, it will be scary. But the decision is in your hands of either facing it and trying or limiting yourself by succumbing to your fear. The beauty of facing it is that it will be terrifying for the first few minutes, uncomfortable and out of place. But slowly, you'd ease into it, you'd feel much better about it and after the experience, you'd feel accomplished. You would have finished your fear. These three F's help you to achieve and gain power over any fear that keeps you limited.

One of my close friends, Harsh, had never been on a road trip. Whenever he tried, he got unwell. He had a phobia of long drives. One day, his father approached him as his mother was ill, and had to go on a doctor's suggested vacation. As much as his father wanted his mother to recover, when he heard about this, Harsh hugged him and started to cry. His mother wished to visit the Dwarkadhish temple and spend some time there. "She can have the vacation. I'll be happy to pay for it," Harsh said. "Thank you, son. Your mother also wants you to come," his father said. "No. I can't get on a drive." His father was disappointed after hearing this and left. The sight of his father leaving didn't bother him. But the dream he had that night did. In his dream, he almost had the same conversation earlier with his father. Although this time, he was talking to his mother. While his mother's words were similar to his father's, his dream had a lasting impact on him. When his mother gently closed the door and left, he felt bothered. When he woke up, he thought about how his mother was always there for him. He recalled the memories of his high school graduation, first job, first bike, first promotion — she was always there. He remembered how she never missed any of the important milestones in his life. And when he wanted anything, even if she couldn't afford it, she was never afraid to find the means to give it to him.

Now it was his turn to be there for her. He rushed to his mother's room, and without thinking twice about his decision, he told his mother he was ready to go with her. His mother smiled and said: "I was sad when you were not coming with us. But knowing about your fear, I was okay with it. But now, I'm happy. Tell me, what made you change your mind?" Harsh told his mother about the dream. He also told her that giving up his fear of driving was the least he could do for her. Shortly after the family vacation at Dwarkadhish, his mother was delighted. From that moment on, he felt nothing but a willingness to see new places.

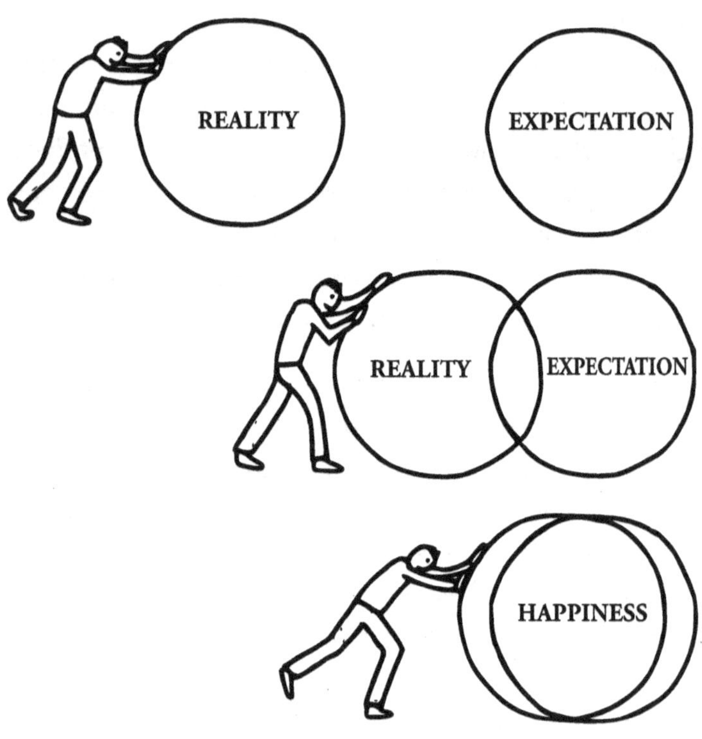

It takes effort to overcome your fear, to bridge your reality with your expectation, but you would realize that only that bridging can make you truly happy.

And from that moment on, he realised his fear of driving didn't have power over him anymore. In a way, his mother gave him the encouragement he needed. If it weren't for that encouragement, he wouldn't have been able to be as satisfied with his life as he is now.

To make life healthy and extraordinary, we must overcome our fear. Have faith in yourself. Do not think less of yourself. God has blessed you with limitless capabilities.

1. List Down The Biggest Fears You Have In Your Life:

   a. ______________________________________

   b. ______________________________________

   c. ______________________________________

   d. ______________________________________

   e. ______________________________________

   f. ______________________________________

   g. ______________________________________

2. List Down The Habits That You Need To Start Practising From Today Which Will Help You In Overcoming Your Fears:

a. ____

b. ____

c. ____

d. ____

e. ____

f. ____

g. ____

Chapter 4

ALIGN AND FOCUS

> *"Focus on your goals, not your fear.*
> *Focus like a laser beam on your goals."*
>
> **~Roy T. Bennett, The Light in the Heart**

ALIGN

Now that we know how we function, the question is, how do we apply this knowledge to our advantage? The answer starts with identifying yourself and your ultimate goal in life and then bridging the two together. Let's acknowledge this step by step and then form a bridge.

Our life is a spectrum of seven components. The wheel of life revolves smoothly when this spectrum is being taken care of in all aspects. This wheel consists of Physical well-being, mental well-being, relationships, time management, career goals, financial stability, celebration, and contribution to society. For each one of us, each of these factors may hold different importance. We may consider two of them except for the others. Maybe one or two factors don't hold any importance for us. But, it is necessary for us to identify their role in our life and to move ahead with a balance of these factors. The balance may not be equally distributed, depending on our priorities.

It may be that you hold your career as the most important factor, in that case it may hold a 60% room in your life, whereas all the other factors may hold a 40% ground altogether. The point is, it is different for each of us, but it is important for us to identify it.

Knowing and accepting yourself for who you are. Spending some time with yourself and introspect using these four tools. Look at your life so far and identify your values, mindset, emotional well-being, and how your state of mind is on a day-to-day basis. You can start by ranking the following in order of the importance you give to each of the following in your life:

1. **Physical well-being**

2. **Mental Well-being**

3. **Relationships**

4. **Time Management**

5. **Career Goals**

6. **Financial Stability**

7. **Celebration and contribution to the society**

Out of the above seven factors, there must be some factors which you give the most importance to and some that you don't hold the place for. However, these factors are what together make a happy and fulfilling life.

You truly align with yourself when you identify your old patterns along with the new patterns you need to adopt and then put them together to transform and be a better version of yourself.

Now think about what areas you need to work harder on. We need to pay more attention to specific areas we're afraid to face or bring change. But we need to realise that these areas are the ones that need our special attention. If we focus and work towards improving them, we'll undoubtedly lead a more prosperous and fulfilling life.

Now, let's take each topic and answer the questions for introspection.

1. **Physical well-being** – Do you eat healthy? Get enough exercise daily? Do you ensure that you get proper sleep each night and are well-rested for the day ahead?

2. **Mental well-being** – How is your mind space? Are you in touch with your feelings? Do you communicate about how you feel? Do you take responsibility for being happy? Does your life make you happy?

3. **Relationships** – Do you have close relationships in your life? How do you determine them to be near? Are those relationships healthy? Can you indeed be yourself in those relationships?

4. **Time management** – Do you make sure that you assign time durations for each task you need to do each day? In your day, do you have time not just for work but also for your relationships, you and the things you love to do? Do you give a lot of time to just one thing and have no time for other aspects of your life?

5. **Career Goals** – What are you pursuing right now? Does it make you happy? Is this the career you had

wanted to follow in life? What is the ultimate goal for you in your career? Are you satisfied with where you are working right now? If not, what would you do instead?

6. **Financial Stability** – Are your finances in order? Do you have enough savings to be secure? Are you happy with what you make? Do you think you can earn more? If yes, then what are your steps towards it?

7. **Celebration and contribution to society** – Do you make it a point to celebrate when you can? Are you also contributing to the community when in need? Are you generous when you need to be?

This exercise aims to, first of all, declutter our life and get organised in our thoughts. The answers you have with you define the areas where you need to work harder, where you're placed well, the areas you feel can be improved and the areas you're happy with. Once we have these things clear with us, there must be a specific area, a specific something that means the most to you. The primary task of this exercise is to identify ourselves. See what we have held as a priority in life and the areas we do not consider necessary.

Think about why it is so? Is this a result of our values, mindset, or emotions? Why are we in the present situation? What factors have led us to be in the current position? This question will help you to get things in perspective. But here, it is essential to:

a. Be honest with ourselves

b. Please take responsibility for the decisions that you've made in life so far. Not taking action is also a decision, and most importantly,

c. Accept yourself for your choices, mistakes, and victories with kindness

After this exercise, you'll have a clearer vision of your life. Now, that you know who you are and what you aspire to become, the main task here is to bridge these together. Once you identify where you ultimately want to be, you must specify the one thing that will take you to your ultimate goal. The goal in our lives is to achieve an extraordinary life. It doesn't mean that we'll continuously stay happy for all our days. It's not possible. It simply means attaining contentment and true happiness through what you do, the people you surround yourself with and the life you build for yourself. The one thing we identify needs to hold extreme importance for us. It is imperative. In order to surrender and align all our efforts towards achieving our ultimate goal in life, we must be incredibly passionate about it.

Every morning when you wake up, try to map out the day ahead of you and every night, when you go to bed, try to analyse your day and your actions. This little self-analysis makes us more aware of the kind of behaviours we want to practise and the type of person we want to become and constantly makes us improve. It is a continuous process. Once we get into a transparent dialogue with ourselves, we start to see what works for us and what doesn't. We need to know if we're happy with the life we have.

If not, what lacks, or what makes us happy? Once we make this a habit, we get a better grip on our lives. We better understand the kind of life we want, the person we want to be, and how we want to shape our lives for the longer term. That vision becomes more apparent as we start looking at our life from the perspective of a second person.

FOCUS

Dronacharya was often asked and questioned by his pupils as to why Arjun was his favourite. Ideally, a teacher is supposed to be unbiased, but when the Kauravs and Pandavs went to his gurukul, Dronacharya had a special inclination towards the third Pandav given his perseverance and dedication. One day, he decided to show everybody the reason behind it, by giving them a task. He placed a wooden bird on a tree branch and assembled all his pupils. He said, "All of you have an archery test today. You need to step forward one by one and aim to strike the wooden bird's eye which I have placed on that tree branch." As Duryodhan stepped ahead and took his stance, Dronacharya asked him to pause and asked him what he could see while aiming. To which he answered, he could see the bird, the branches, leaves, and trees. Dronacharya asked him to step aside. As each pupil stepped forward one by one, he asked everyone the same question. Each of them had various answers, like the bird, the trees, the surroundings, etc. Eventually, it was Arjun's turn. Dronacharya asked him the same question, only to get an answer that no one had given so far. Arjun said he could only see the bird's eye. Only and only the bird's eye. Proud after hearing his answer, Dronacharya let him proceed ahead and Arjun was able to hit the target.

Arjun is known to be the greatest archer
in the world not just because of his aim,
but because of his FOCUSED AIM.

It was not about how skilled Arjun was at archery, but it was because of how focused he was that he was able to hit the given target. This was exactly what Dronacharya wanted to show everyone as to why Arjun was his favourite. All the pupils of the gurukul had the same classes and received the same knowledge and time to practise, but it was his undeniably strong focus that made him stand apart from everyone else. This is the power of being focused. If you want to achieve anything in life, a stable focus is an absolute necessity.

Time is the same for all of us. We all get 24 hours in a day, then why do only a limited number of us are able to achieve bigger and higher goals? Why are some people able to get done with significantly more tasks as compared to others? The answer is simple, it depends completely on what quantum we are focused on to achieve. It depends on what we aim at and how focused we are to achieve it. Amongst various tasks to be done in an entire day, it is necessary for us to set our priorities and get them done in a focused manner. We need to identify the things which matter the most to us and work on them with dedication. If your aim is to get fit, you need to work out and follow a diet religiously. You need to make it a priority. You need to figure out the exercise which works for you, and your calorie intake and balance it with the rest your body needs. You'll need to be mindful of avoiding junk food and extra carbs.

You'll need to be mindful of various factors which would have an impact on your physical health and keep moving forward with dedication, discipline and clarity.

Good distraction

Bad distraction

Re-energise and reboot
after focussed work

An escape path from the
thing we are trying to avoid

> *Often, instead of focusing on a very important task, we tend to get distracted and divulge into bad distractions which do us no good. Taking a break with good thing is productive, but procrastination is pointless.*

Being productive doesn't mean being busy all the time doing multiple tasks, it means spending a dedicated amount of time on tasks that focus on achieving something significant and meaningful. Things that serve a bigger purpose. The purpose is your focus. But does this mean that focused continuous efforts at a straight length would produce immediate results? No. In this case, starving yourself for days or working out extremely for a day will not help you achieve your target, rather these efforts will go to waste. As they say, Rome was not built in a day. The important thing is to consistently make dedicated efforts each day to achieve the desired result. When we have a balanced, dedicated approach to things, we are able to maintain a balance amongst all aspects of our lives and also achieve our goals.

Follow

One

Course

Until

Successful

We have limited time and energy. If we spend our time and energy on doing various menial things at once, it will not lead us to any productive results and we would only waste our time and energy. It is important that we allocate our energies and time to quality tasks that will contribute to achieving our ultimate goals and not just stay productive for the sake of staying productive.

If we don't align our work and tasks in a synchronised manner with our ultimate goal, we will never be able to achieve our dreams and will not be able to cope with our lives and circumstances. We need to primarily decide and set our focus on the one primary thing we need to achieve in our life. That thing is our ultimate goal towards which we must plan and take productive actions. When we know how we want our life to be ultimately in each aspect, we would automatically find it easy to plan and align our tasks, actions, and most primarily mind, towards achieving it every day.

Many of us just start doing things without setting out our priorities for the day straight. Everything that comes to our mind seems to be equally important to us and we forget to value our tasks as per their real priorities. This resulted in us not being able to achieve the things which were more important because we ended up wasting our time on things that could have been left for later or could have been delegated. It is important to prioritise and plan things in order to have efficient working productivity.

For example, when we think about going on a vacation, we consider various things step by step. We think about where we want to go, when will it be possible for us to take a break, the duration, the necessary travel arrangements, hotel bookings, places to see, dedicating a number of days to each destination, etc. according to how we want to travel. This would make a nice and blissful vacation where you would feel happy and energised. Similarly, if every day we could plan our tasks, and chores accordingly and achieve them, we would feel more productive, happy and satisfied. We need to concentrate completely on one thing at a time. If you're in the gym for one hour, you need to focus and work out with a complete body, mind, and soul. If you're delivering a lecture in college, you need to be completely present and interactive in that session. When you're playing with your dog, you need to focus on your dog and the quality time you spend with him.

Multitasking with everything at once doesn't let us achieve anything solid. We are mere human beings, not Gods. We can do things one by one in a dedicated manner and with our best effort. We lose our focus when we attempt to multitask and our aim doesn't appear clear to us. We need to be strong-willed and committed to our tasks. At a lot of points in our daily lives, we think about achieving an excessive number of tasks in a day. We think we'll be able to accommodate everything and achieve everything without being practical.

This is also one of the reasons why when someone who might be close to us, comes forward with a task for us and we start doing it, leaving everything that we were supposed to do. Instead of seeing when we can do it comfortably, we succumb to it and don't end up achieving our targets for the day. This practice becomes extremely negative for us and we are not able to do our work.

It is extremely important for us to prioritise our work and value ourselves. It is extremely important to first gauge if we can accommodate and help out when and if we can. But if we can't, it is very necessary to say no. Saying no is as important as aiming to achieve your goals. Only by drawing true and realistic boundaries, will you be able to truly value yourself and your time. A true no is any day better than a false yes or succumbing to helping others at the cost of our own time and energy.

Now List Out What is Your Ultimate Objective For Each of The Following Areas of Your Life And List Them.

Physical Well being:

Mental Well being:

Balancing Relationships:

Time Management:

Career Goals:

Financial Stability:

Celebration And Contributing To The Society:

Reflect on today. Life is a combination of moments. Each moment, each day, comes together to make our life. But how much do we actually value each passing moment? Do we realise this? Let's analyse our life and see how much we contribute to each day.

Daily Layout			
Time	Tasks	Ritual Tasks And Their Importance	
4:00 AM			
5:00 AM			
6:00 AM			
7:00 AM			
8:00 AM			
9:00 AM			

10:00 AM		Meal Schedule	
11:00 AM			
NOON			
1:00 PM			
2:00 PM			
3:00 PM			
4:00 PM			
5:00 PM		Physical	
6:00 PM		Activity	
7:00 PM		Schedule	
8:00 PM			
9:00 PM			
10:00 PM			
11:00 PM			
Midnight			

After looking at your schedule above, ponder over how you can become more focused and better at your daily tasks. Identify and write down the areas where you need to be more focused and the areas where you need to take a step back from investing too much of your time in.

Areas In Need of More Attention And Action	Areas That Don't Need So Much of Your Attention

Areas In Need of More Attention And Action Areas That Don't Need So Much of Your Attention.

Chapter 5

SMART WORK

> *"Until you value yourself, you won't value your time. Until you value your time, you will not do anything with it."*
>
> ~M. Scott Pe

One thing my grandfather used to say very often that I never understood was, 'Life is too short to not do what you want'. I could never comprehend what he was trying to tell me when I was younger. But, today I know what he meant. What he was always trying to tell me was the value of time and to learn to value time. Time is limited, time doesn't stop. The clock keeps ticking and time flies. It evaporates like water in the heat. I remember, he would always say "You can get everything back in life, relationships, material things, you could buy things, borrow things, but you cannot turn back time." When we realise it, often we get too late. It is very important to understand the value of each and every passing second for each and every one of us.

When we were growing up, all of us had a set timetable for us to follow and hence we had a habit of getting our tasks done in a set time frame. Everything was scheduled for us. We had a set timeline from getting up in the morning, getting ready for school, having breakfast, reaching school, attending all the classes, having lunch break, going back home, doing homework, play time in the evening, having dinner, and finally, going to bed. By following this set routine only, we could get done with each task on time.

It was because of that discipline only, that we could be happy in life and enjoy childhood in all aspects possible. But unfortunately, as we grow older, we lose that sense of discipline and value for time. We do not have a set schedule for the short term or for the long term. We do not sleep or wake up at a scheduled time. We don't have set eating hours and we don't draw a line between our work hours and the hours we need to dedicate to our personal life. When we do not have a fixed routine or schedule, then how can we achieve what we want?

Most of today's young generation doesn't have a set time to go to bed, most of the youngsters believe in pulling all-nighters. They have become night owls who work and stay up through the night and sleep through at least half of the entire day. Then how can we maintain discipline at all when we are going against nature? When there is no discipline, then we cannot achieve success or happiness in our life. Today we are living in the world of technology. We can do multiple things in a matter of minutes, unlike in the past. Everything used to be manual in the past days, for example, maintaining accounts records, doing household work, etc. Today, technology has become an integral part of our daily life. It has made our work easy and time efficient.

Balance is the Key to making a happy life. It is the wisest to maintain it.

Even after this, we are unable to maintain a healthy balance between our personal and professional life. We do not have time for our parents, or children, life partners, to work with concentration or even for our physical health. Then where is all this time flying? Have you ever evaluated? If you think about it, you will see that lots of time is wasted on useless and unproductive work, and we do not even realise it. Most of our time goes engrossed in our phones, ipads, or laptops. People don't realise that most of their time is spent scrolling through social media, following people and pages we don't know, watching useless reels and videos, and chatting with those who are not even significant in our lives.

Today we have many resources, but instead of using them to our advantage, we just use them as a mode of entertainment or to pass our time. This makes us addicted, lazy, and extremely unproductive. It comes to a point that we do not want to make any effort to fulfil our dreams. What is it that we need to do in this case? Continue to fall deep into this never-ending trap and waste our time away, or do we need to find a way to stop and take control of our time and our lives? Let's get a grip, make our minds strong, and take control in our own hands.

It is by continuous efforts each day that we are able to refine and define our goals.

Early to bed, early to rise.

This simple rule holds a deep-rooted value. It has great significance and has held true for centuries. Our elders have continuously emphasised getting up very early in the morning and starting the daily routine. Everyone who is successful begins their day very early. Why? Because they know the importance of getting up early and beginning their day. What is this importance? If we get up by 4:00 am, we have sufficient time for ourselves. We have time to organise and plan our day. We have time to be with our families, we have time to be with ourselves and organise our thoughts, and practise our health regimes. After getting up early in the morning and getting done with these things, we can plan our day with our mind aligned. We get enough time to think about the solutions for the challenges that we may have, we can build a working plan for the taks we need to get done during the day so that all we have to do is take action. We can plan for the future and see what is the next step we need to take for us to be where we want to be. We can give time to our interests, we can also follow a regular health regime, and when everything is done timely, we live in a fulfilled and content state of mind happily.

If your work day starts at about 9:00 am, and you get up by seven. How much time do you get to plan your day? After doing the necessary tasks to get ready and eating breakfast, you won't even get half an hour to align your mind with your actions. How do you plan your day in this case? How will you tread towards the bright future you want?

> *It is the small acts of discipline that lead to true success. Excuses keep you stuck.*

Now, if you start the same day at 4:00 or even 5:00 am, you have five to four hours to do everything. You can wake up very calmly. You can work out, meditate, and can plan your day with alignment. You can think of ways of tackling your challenges ahead with a calm approach and make plans for a better and brighter future. Surprisingly, you will do all this very calmly and with complete focus. Why? Because you are aligned with yourself. The time you spend with yourself in such hours, are just yours with no disturbances or distractions.

Successful people make it a point to get up early in the morning. Firstly, they know that this is the time they can spend on their own without any commitments. They can pay attention to their physical and mental health by working out, meditating, and spending time on spirituality or on their interests, whereas ordinary people won't have the time and will spend their days rushing here and there in an unorganised manner.

Secondly, successful people know that by getting up early in the morning, they have extra four hours to work on various aspects, which can lead them to success.

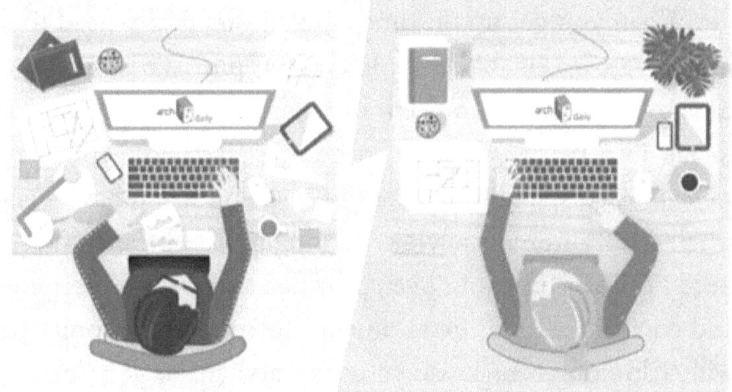

Keeping to the point and making
your surroundings organized,
organizes your mind.

During those hours, they plan their meetings according to priority, they strategies on matters that need their undivided attention, formulate solutions to issues that are going on, revise their to-do lists, and think over new ideas to maintain their position and grow further ahead from it. They create their daily set targets, and to achieve them, they set their day accordingly and achieve what their target is.

When you get up on time, you automatically need to get to bed at a reasonable hour, like 10:00 pm. When we set the time to wake up and to sleep, automatically our schedule starts to fall into place. We need to be home by 7:00 pm so that we can relax, spend time with our loved ones and have a good meal. This automatically starts bringing the balance that we need in all aspects of our lives, provided that we stay disciplined and committed. This extra time in the morning automatically will help you to organise your day and make your personal and professional life in harmony.

Now, let's have a look at the time schedule of a typical day in the lives of Mr. Kapadia, a businessman.

MR. KAPADIA'S	
4:00 AM	Wake up, Get fresh
4:30 AM	Reviews to do list of previous day, reply to mails
5:00 AM	Ponder on the solutions to the challenges, revise the to do list.
6:30 AM	Spend some times for hobbies
7:00AM	Go to gym
8:30 AM	Tea time, reads newspaper
9:00 AM	Having breakfast, Getting to the once and planning the entire day

This way, if we make it a habit to get up early every day, we can get a significant amount of work done before going to the office. So when our actual work day begins, we can do our work very calmly, and happily and can actually enjoy it. When we are ready with the necessary solutions to our problems and have everything according to our schedule, then it will also motivate the people working for us to achieve their targets within the time limit, and ultimately, you are successful.

It is the point of view that matters.
Only managing your time, can make
your challenges to opportunities.

Block your time

We need to achieve a lot of milestones to fulfil our dreams, for the happiness of our family and most importantly, ours. We have only twenty-four hours a day, seven days a week, about 30 days a month, and 365 days a year. But we get intimidated by our long to-do list and get nothing done. Now the question is, how do we do this?

What can we do to achieve all the milestones we want and live happily?

Time blocking is the tool that will help us achieve exactly this. After getting up early in the morning, plan your day. How will you start your day? Write down your plan, from the moment you get up to the point of going to bed. Similarly, plan your week, month, and year. This way, you will be able to block your calendar. The minute you make things tangible, tasks become achievable. All your work, meetings, and travelling will be scheduled accordingly, and you will see that you can focus on all aspects of your life, whether it's your health, spirituality, personal life, or professional life. You can balance your life. This is how you will be able to accomplish important tasks productively instead of doing a big quantity of work that does not reap any tangible results.

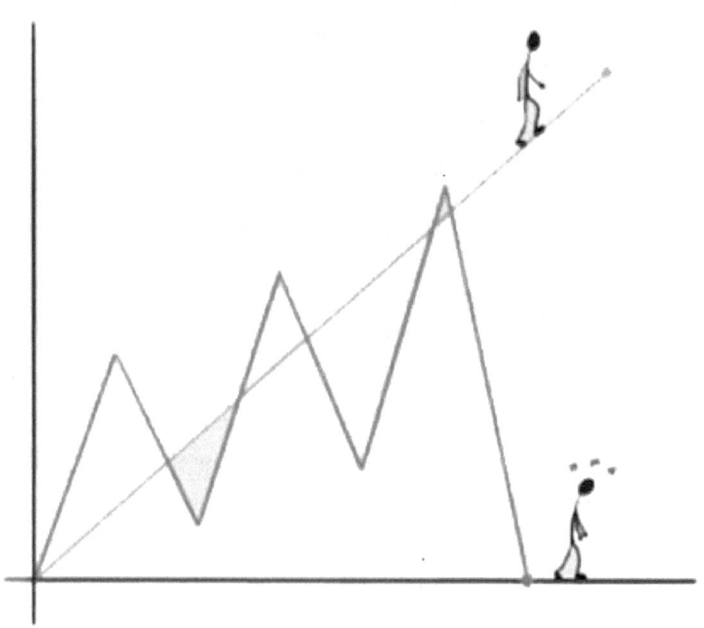

Once we build a bridge between our time with our habits and motivation, we motivation, we move towards success.

Most successful people make their plans at the beginning of the year. They know the importance and value of their time and do not waste it. Time is more valuable than anything, even money.

You can always make money, you can find ways to do that but if time runs out, you can never get it back.

By setting your daily schedule, you get enough time to manage your resources, and in turn, you also save time for those you are connected to. When you fix an appointment with someone, they set their other meetings or tasks around that time. It causes a dominoes effect impacting the time schedule of people they have set their tasks and appointments with. If you or they don't stick to the schedule responsibly, it affects and wastes not only the time but even the opportunities of all those multiple people who are connected.

This is a lesson I learned the hard way. I was not so punctual when I started out. It was normal for me to get late to meetings and I didn't value 15-20 mins. One day I had an important meeting with a very significant customer for a crucial deal that could have rocketed my growth exponentially. As usual, I was half an hour late, and I kept the client waiting. When I finally made it, we could only have the meeting for the time which was left out of the time he had assigned for me. I was surprised, it had never happened to me. When I asked him for extra time, he refused to say the exact same thing. He couldn't hamper his schedule because of my mistake. I lost my deal. That was a tough lesson that made me realise the value of time. Since that day, I have made sure to use my time in a disciplined manner.

WORK HARDER   WORK SMARTER

Just working hard keeps us stuck in a loop. But working smarter, makes us climb the ladder of success.

We can get enough time to interact with our parents, our spouses, and our children. When we organise our day and work accordingly, we can live a happy and fulfilling life. We share our lives in a well- connected manner and build our experiences. This becomes a strong source of happiness, contentment, and strength for us and our loved ones.

If we plan well, we can actually block our time and justify and fulfil all the areas of our life. When we go from macro to micro, our goals become achievable. Let's go through the templates and make things feasible for you.

Yearly Planing												
	Jan.	Feb.	Mar.	Apr.	May	June	July	Aug.	Sept.	Oct.	Nov.	Dec.
Physical Well Being												
Mental Well Being												
Relation Balance												
Time Management												
Career Goals												
Financial Goals												
Celebration												

Monthly Planner: January				
	WEEK 1	WEEK 2	WEEK 3	WEEK 4
Physical Well Being				
Mental Well Being				
Relation Balance				
Time Management				
Career Goals				
Financial Goals				
Celebration				

Weekly Planner: January, Week 1							
	MON	TUE	WED	THUR	FRI	SAT	SUN
Physical Well Being							
Mental Well Being							
Relation Balance							
Time Management							
Career Goals							
Financial Goals							
Celebration							

Daily Planner: Monday							
	Physical Well Being	Mental Well Being	Relation Balance	Time Management	Career Goals	Financial Goals	Celebration
4:00 AM							
5:00 AM							
6:00 AM							
7:00 AM							
8:00 AM							
9:00 AM							
10:00 AM							
11:00 AM							
12 Noon							
1:00 PM							
2:00 PM							
3:00 PM							
4:00 PM							
5:00 PM							
6:00 PM							
7:00 PM							
8:00 PM							
9:00 PM							
10:00 PM							
11:00 PM							

Build your strength

When we were small kids, we were fearless and curious to try everything. But as we grew up, we became more conscious and calculated in how we move forward. We develop our choices, our likes, and dislikes. We love to do things according to our preferences in every aspect, whether it is related to studies, recreation, or friends. We love to do only what we feel comfortable with or have confidence in. Things that we like to do become our strengths, and anything which is new to us or beyond our comfort zone, we find it very difficult to cope with and claim as our weakness.

In earlier times, children were only supposed to do what was told by their parents no matter what their interests were. As a result, their efforts were only aligned with instruction and not a well-thought-out aim. This resulted in mediocrity and not being able to achieve the success that they wanted. But now things have changed. Now the relationship between parents and their children has changed and the views of kids are also taken into account while making important decisions. This helps in the results being more successful as they are not forced and have been made with interests and likes and dislikes. This automatically makes everyone happier and more content and the results are also extraordinary.

Sometimes I get confused about whether I should make efforts to improve my weaknesses or strengthen my strength. This is probably a struggle that most of us struggle with on a daily basis. One day when my guru ji visited us, I asked him about this dilemma, and he answered this very simply. He said, no one is perfect in this world. We should focus on what we are good at and for the things that are not our strengths, we can seek the help of those who are good at them. We alone can not do everything, it's impossible. We can be good in some areas but not in everything. When we seek help and connect with those who will be able to help us, not only do we connect with more resources, but we also are able to work in a relaxed manner and more efficiently. In life to attain success we need good people who can help us to achieve our goals. If we have a good team then our targets can be achieved within a good time limit.

Suppose you have a team of 100 people out of which only 20% people give tangible output, you can still achieve your goal. The reason is how we think differently here and focus only on those 20% people. If our focus remains on the remaining 80% who do not produce results, our time, money, and resources will go in vain and we won't be able to achieve what we desire.

A principle called '80/20' has proven that 80% of output flows from 20% of resources. This principle states that a concentrated combination of small actions leads to major outputs. A student who studies continuously for more than twelve hours to prepare for exams may not get first position in his class, but a student who doesn't study at such lengths is able to achieve the desired result. Why is that so? The first student did not analyse what he needed to study, didn't prioritise, and just continued to do unorganised expected actions. On the other hand, the other student analysed and planned the topics he needed to study well. He planned properly and strategized efficiently and achieved his desired result. Similarly, in business, if you have ten types of products and among those three are more profitable, you need to focus on those three products primarily. Instead of doing too much and not achieving what you want, make your efforts targeted and achieve more significantly.

Focus on the resources or efforts that give you more profitability rather than the ones which require more energy, time, and money and don't reap any results. Target a limited number from a wide variety of valuable opportunities rather than pursuing every available opportunity. This will not only waste your time, money, and energy but it will also not help you achieve your dreams.

We need to know and accept that we cannot master everything in this world, we cannot be perfect. Everyone has their own strengths and their own expertise. The power of your strength is probably different from that of the others. It is impossible to learn everything at once because it will just confuse us and it will not be fruitful. It is better to master one or several things which are considered important or necessary for us. Unfortunately, many people like to compare themselves to everyone's strengths and want to be able to do everything. They always underestimate themselves and see their weakness rather than their strength.

Remember, The Power of Your Strengths. Focus on your strengths. Do not compare yourself with anyone else. Use your strength to your benefit. Never think of yourself as inferior or weaker than anyone else. This will hamper your self-esteem immensely. Increase your self-esteem by assimilating your strengths and always improving so that you are better and stronger than ever before.

1. To actually make your goals achievable, now you need to plan your life, yourself. Use the templates of the year, month, week, and day to make your goals tangible for you and see your life transform.

2. Now to know yourself better and to become more efficient and achieve better results. We all have strengths and weaknesses, the point is to identify them, be aware of them, and act accordingly. Now, list down your strengths and weaknesses so that you can identify them for yourself and hold pride in your strengths and work smartly around your weaknesses.

Strengths	Weaknesses

Chapter 6

THE POWER OF RELATIONSHIPS

> *"Being deeply loved by someone gives you strength while loving someone deeply gives you courage."*
>
> **– Lao-Tzu.**

Since I was a little child, I had been very close to my grandfather. Naturally, I got the values that he imparted to me and have been with them throughout my life. He always used to insist on the importance of maintaining healthy relationships with people. He was a very social person, someone who was loved by one and all, hence he knew the true value of relationships and the people he was connected to.

There was always a sense of strong unity in the entire family dynamic because of him. He was a very successful businessman and a people person. To date, we are renowned as "Jhandewalas" which is his legacy. It is because of his success and goodwill that is known through the masses, that people immediately recognise us when we introduce ourselves. He always believed that no one can survive alone. Maybe you can survive but you cannot live happily on your own, you always need people. To be better, to achieve something in life, we need support. Relationships are the strong foundations on which life is lived with every joy and challenge.

*A happy home and good relationships
build a good life full of growth and love.*

I used to love hearing his stories, they were always fun and he loved telling little anecdotes. I remember one such piece that I still hold very close. A small kid was strolling in the woods with his father. As they were struggling along, they came across a huge tree that had fallen in the storm, its trunk blocking the way. Curious as the child was, he asked his father if he thought he'd be able to lift that trunk. His father responded with strong reassurance, saying 'Why not? You can lift it if you utilise your power!'

The little kid tried to do the same, trying to put all his energy to lift the trunk, but he couldn't. Disappointed, he said, "No dad, I am not powerful enough." Smiling, his father encouraged him to try it again. The child tried to do it again, but the result was the same. Disheartened again, he said to his father, "See! I am not able to do this, I don't have it in me." His father smiled and told him, "Son, I asked you to utilise all your power, but you didn't." Confused, the child didn't understand what he meant. His father continued, "you never asked for me to add to your efforts, even when you knew I was right here to help you!" The kid smiled and looked at his father fondly. Both of them put their efforts together and were able to remove the tree trunk out of their way, and headed further into the woods happily.

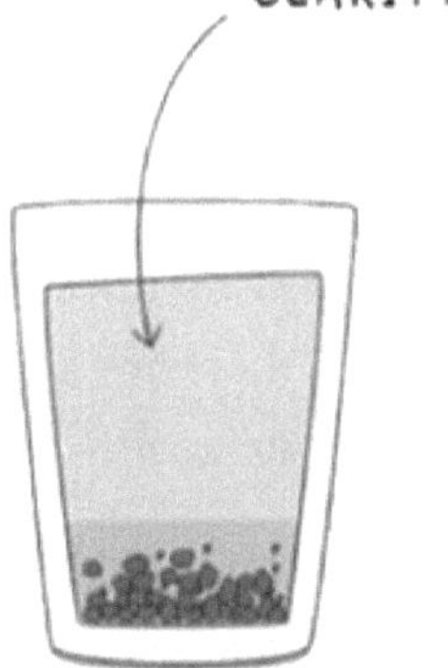

When we are just involved with ourselves,
we keep getting mixed with only our thoughts.
Stepping back and seeking advice and help, bring
us a nice pause and a much needed clarity.

The moral of this story is that we need to trust our loved ones. If we think we can do everything just by ourselves and do not need any help from the people around us, we are highly mistaken. When we ask for help, it doesn't mean that we are incapable of handling the situation, it means that we would definitely be able to overcome challenges of any magnitude if we seek help from our loved ones. They don't only become our physical and mental strength, but they also give our morale a boost. The zeal to solve problems and overcome challenges pumps up highly. We need to realise, acknowledge and appreciate the support, strength, and importance of the people who are there for us, who love us, and who are with us to achieve our goals.

Our real strength resides in these dynamics that we share with our people. No person is sufficient to achieve all goals. Not just one person can have all the talents and qualities. We need resources to grow, prosper and make our vision a reality. It is wise to seek people out for guidance and support in the areas which are not our expertise so that we can get the best advice and excel ahead. People are our biggest resources.

Collaborations and associations are the way to move forward. They are the symbol of greater strength and power. We must continue to persevere for important collaborations. When we are seeking assistance and are denied, it just indicates that we need to make another request at another time, in a different manner, or to a different person. We need to improve our persuasion skills. We need to keep in mind the 'SWs'. Some Will, Some Won't, but it doesn't matter because someone is still waiting.

> *You cannot construct the whole building by yourself! It's a strong willed team you need! So why shy away? Go and Ask Ahead! Make your dream team, become stronger and Conquer the World!*

Similarly, it does not matter how much knowledge we have, we need people with us who are competent to realise our goals. When we find ourselves in a situation where we cannot move forward, we need someone with whom we can discuss our concerns, take some guidance, and a correct direction. If we want to be successful in life, we need the assistance of a good team that is capable enough of fully comprehending our vision and is aligned to help us achieve our objectives and realise our goals.

A car runs on four tires. Similarly, if we want to have a happy life and see our aspirations come true, we need the cohesive support and assistance of other people who are knowledgeable in the relevant fields. On the other hand, we also need to be there to assist people who would need our assistance and expertise in the areas they may lack in. We need to work on developing positive relationships. Healthy relationships motivate us when we fall short, provide reassurance when we are unsure, and stay present to share our joy when we succeed.

We can forge strong connections with one another by doing important things and standing strong with one another throughout the process. You can show the ones you are connected with, how much you care by letting them know how important they are to your life and how much you value them. Even in the professional world, it is not necessary to only maintain objective relationships. Healthy and amicable relationships can be made and maintained with the people that you have worked with and the ones you continue to work with. Relationships are like roses, they are sensitive and beautiful. You need to water them, take care of them, and nurture them for them to keep living and blooming.

You may have collaborated with someone at some point in your life. Or you may have known them very well professionally but have lost touch now. If today, you are in the middle of a challenge and are unable to solve some issue, or if new opportunities arise in which you get reminded that they are the ones who can help you out, you must reach out to them. Why? Because you had an excellent relationship with them. Even when you may not have any work terms presently, you always attempted to help them in trying times. Profit and loss come secondary to maintaining relationships. It should be upheld with an unwavering commitment and trust. Calling someone solely because you need their time to reflect a self-centred attitude.

Thinking of them, and keeping them in good thoughts while things were going well for them demonstrates brilliance and positivity. If you have a friend that you haven't seen for ages and run into him unexpectedly and you know the good things that have been going well for him and you congratulate him and talk to him about it, it will only leave positivity and goodness in his mind for you. You never know who, or where might need you or may touch your life unexpectedly. People may come and go in a blink of an eye, you can never predict it, so it is always a good thing to spread positivity around you and for the people around you.

Sometime back, my wife and I were to make a work trip to Guwahati. A day before I remembered I had a school friend Manish who was based there. We hadn't been in touch for several years, but I couldn't help but give him a call. I ultimately did, and we decided to meet. When my wife asked how close we were, I told her that we had never been that close ever, but it is a nice thought to go and meet. My wife was shocked. She insisted as to why bother some long lost friends when you're not even that close and haven't met for so long! But I just couldn't help it. To both our surprise, Manish and his wife gave us a warm welcome and became great hosts. We shared our experiences of the old school days, video called all school friends and went back in time together. After not being in touch for so long, everyone was happily surprised to have gotten back in touch. It was a trip worth remembering. My wife, too, was surprised. She said, "if I would have seen you two together like this without any context, I could have never guessed that you have not been in touch for almost 10-15 years now!"

Once, my wife and I decided to go on a vacation on a cruise in Alaska. As we prepared to embark on the trip, I began to feel uneasy and ultimately decided to turn around. I felt extremely uncomfortable, so I asked my agent to transfer my bookings to some other hotel at some other destination.

But for various reasons, nothing could be formulated. We considered various activities to engage in for the weeklong trip on the cruise, but I was constantly anxious. One day, we met a couple who were originally from Kanpur and began to talk by the pool. Within a few hours, we were able to form a good connection and became good friends till today. After that trip, we ran into them in 2023, after almost 13 years. Even though we speak on the phone every once in a while, it always feels much closer than we are geographically whenever we do. There is a strong bond between the two of us.

I have learned the value of maintaining healthy connections from my grandfather, it is not something that is only limited to my close connections but I practise this even in my professional relationships.

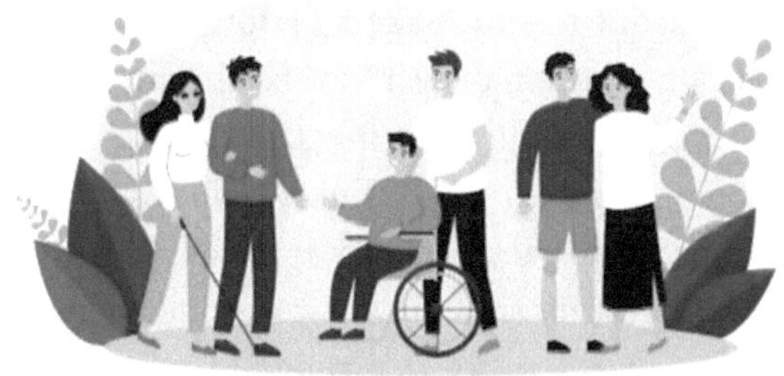

Healthy
Relationships

> *Building healthy relationship with everyone is the key to a fulfilling life. It has so much to offer!*

I don't usually get to the point and only maintain a formal decorum, instead, I like to make an effort to connect with the other person on a personal level too. For instance, asking them about their health, family, business, etc. After asking about their well-being, I get to the business point of view. At times, even if we are unable to reach an agreement, I will continue to uphold our relationship, I will continue to maintain our relationship. I always make it a point to wish them well on special occasions like birthdays, anniversaries, and holidays so that I can include them in my joy. Sending them presents on holidays and other noteworthy occasions are also some of how I continue to embrace the relationship.

Not only does this motivate me and make my life happier and richer, but it also makes them feel special. They get to feel that we are also a part of their joy and experiences in their lives. It is extremely important to also create a positive and wholesome atmosphere at work and with the people you work with. Following are a few simple changes, which may help in creating that:

- By recognising and appreciating the efforts of the staff members. Honouring the groups that have successfully completed their goals, and so on.

- Employees who have put in the effort but are still unable to meet their goals need to be motivated.

- Relationships that are both healthy and productive between employees and employers.

- Giving them access to the appropriate tools and encouraging them to share their ideas is one approach to providing support while they work through their challenges.

- We maintain positive and healthy ties with the people working for us as well. It is with their assistance, that we will be able to reach our goals.

When we go through highs and lows in our lives, we tend to take most aspects of our personal lives for granted. As we progress along the road to success, our daily schedules are packed. But we need to remember that someone is waiting for us at the dinner table. We are unable to spend good time with our children, our parents, or any of our other family members. We don't give any of those relationships a second thought. At a lot of points, when we want our family members to be with us, they might not don't have time for us. Disagreements, quarrels, and feelings of disappointment begin to emerge more frequently in relationships over time when we are unable to concentrate on the goals we have set for ourselves. We are not capable of completing any assignment satisfactorily.

As a direct consequence of this, we can never be successful. Consequently, leading a happy and successful life requires a strong foundation in personal relationships as well. When we are at ease, when our needs are met, and when we are content, we can concentrate on our work and be more productive. In most cases, my Guru ji advises that everything related to work should remain at the workplace. It cannot tag along with you wherever you go.

Building relationships requires a significant mental and emotional energy investment. It is natural for us to feel emotional, but it should not be overpowering. We need to maintain a good balance. When we are primarily driven by too much emotion, we lose a sense of what is good and wrong. We may be aware if a certain person is acting inappropriately, but sometimes due to our feelings, we tend to ignore them which may lead to difficulties in our life or the inability to accomplish our objectives. Highly emotional people tend to make decisions based on their preferences rather than on what is rationally right for the situation they are in.

The ego has no place in relationships with anyone. Be it coworkers, employees, or family members.

Relationships are ego-free zones. A person who is very concerned with themselves cannot think clearly. When we are driven by ego, we sometimes lose what we had, and by the time we figure it out, it's too late.

I myself get very emotional, which sometimes makes it hard for me to make decisions and because of this, I've occasionally had to lose good employees who were very important to me. Sometimes I've missed out on good opportunities, which I regret, but as I've said before, time that has passed cannot be turned back.

Relationships should be taken care of like a mother takes care of her child, Whether they are with employees, friends, business partners, or family members. There needs to be mutual love. respect, care, and sincerity, to even have the guts to scold when the other one makes a mistake. No one should have a bias. They need to be handled with care.

But at the end of the day, we must also know that we need to strike a balance between how we project ourselves and deal with our relationships. Getting too personal in a professional connection and staying too formal in a personal relationship are not great practices to have. There should always be a thin line that is kept and respected to keep things civil. If we can strike a healthy balance between our personal and professional lives, we will experience greater levels of happiness and will be better positioned to realise and live up to our full potential.

Now Let's Bring A Balance In Your Life. Let's Analyse How You Do And How You Should See Your Relationships When It Comes To Your Professional And Personal Life.

1. List Down The Practises You Need To Incorporate To Maintain A Healthy Balance Between You And Your Staff Members

    a.

    b.

    c.

2. What Amendments Do You Need To Make At Your Workplace To Ensure A Healthy Work Environment

    a.

    b.

    c.

    d.

    e.

3. List Down The Steps You Need To Take To Make A Better And Healthier Network Professionally With Your Fellow Competitors?

a.

b.

c.

d.

e.

4. How Much Time Do You Spend With Your Family Daily?

5. How Often Would You Like It To Be To Make The Current Situation Better?

6. How Often Do You Meet Your Friends?

7. How Often Would You Like It To Be To Make The Current Situation Better?

8. How Often Do You Go On Vacations?

9. How Often Would You Like It To Be To Make The Current Situation Better?

Think About It. Your Professional Goals, The Money You Make, And The Success You Achieve, Are Not Even Half As Fulfilling If You Don't Have Any Significant People To Share It With, If You Don't Have People Who Have Stood With You While You Struggled, The Ones You Have Supported Through Their Journeys. People Are Your Biggest Resource, The Biggest Comfort. If You Have Been Taking Them For Granted, Wake Up. Wake Up Now, And Tell Them You Love Them And You Appreciate Them. Life Is Too Short To Have Regrets.

Chapter 7

THE POWER OF BELIEF

> *"As you sow is your subconscious mind, so shall you reap in your body and environment."*
>
> **- Dr. Joseph Murphy**

Often I wonder how come only a limited number of people are successful in their life while others struggle on a daily basis for even the basics. Some people like Elon Musk, Mark Zuckerberg, etc, have quickly become millionaires, while some spend their whole lives fulfilling their tiniest wishes. Is this only destiny, or is there another magic that conspires in our lives to help us achieve the things we wish for? Yes, there is magic that is above all of us, it is 'The power of our subconscious mind'. There is a very famous dialogue you must have heard Sharukh Khan say, in the movie Om Shanti Om, *"Agar kisi cheez ko puri shiddat se chaho, toh puri kayanaat usse aapse milvane ki saazish me lag jaati hai"*. Translating to, If you want something from a true and pure heart, the entire universe conspires to make it your reality.

You may wonder though, is it true? And if it is, how does it work? Our brain has two sections: the conscious mind, and the subconscious mind. Your conscious mind is what works actively as per your present thought process and what you grasp from your reality. It consists of what you know at any given point in time. Our conscious mind is completely aware of exactly what we are doing and thinking.

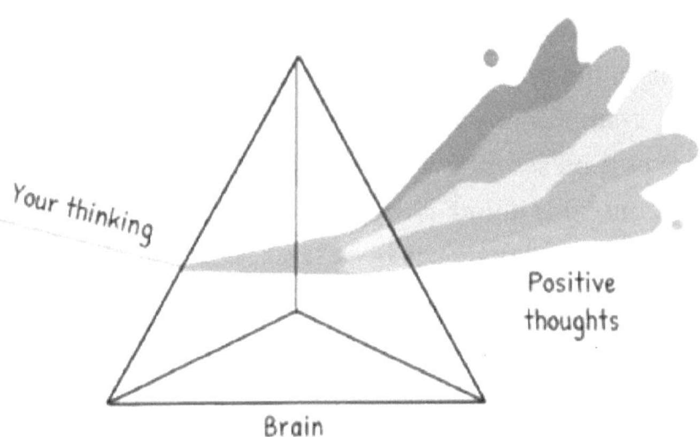

> *It is only what you feed to the prism of your subconscious which will make your life what it is. If you keep making positive thoughts a habit, your life will be no less than a rainbow.*

Whereas, the subconscious mind is the source of our dreams and desires. It serves as a repository for our life experiences and thoughts. It resembles a garden where a gardener has planted seeds. You may not be completely aware of the process of its growth, but you'll know for sure when it reaps the fruits. Everything that you are aware of in all your senses, is what your conscious mind perceives. The conversations you have, the music you listen to, or the information you read are all examples of your conscious mind at work. Your mind's aware portion serves as a doorway to your subconscious mind. Your conscious mind is responsible for thinking, while the subconscious is influenced by it. It takes the conscious thoughts as seeds and sews them and further, acts on them. As a result of this process being simultaneous, the thoughts that run through our heads have an immediate impact on the events that occur in real life.

Whatever our beliefs are, they will have the same effect on our subconscious mind. If we have positive thoughts, then beautiful things will come into our life. On the other hand, if majorly our thoughts are negative, then we will automatically attract bad things. Our subconscious mind uses syllogism based on logic and any conclusions that are to come from it will always stand true, no matter how crazy they seem. For example, if I tell myself that I can't do something because I'm not smart enough or strong enough, but I do know deep inside, that it's not the truth, there's no reason why it should be.

My subconscious will believe me. If you accept a significant premise as true, then any conclusions that will follow from it, will also become valid, no matter how crazy they seem. My subconscious mind will make sure that it starts being true, and ultimately will lead to me becoming, incompetent or weaker than I actually am.

Our subconscious mind is responsible for the majority of our thoughts. If my thoughts arc positive and my belief is strong, no one can stop me from achieving what I want. Once, my friend told me about a new car that Volvo had launched. He took me for a test drive of the same. I was highly impressed with the safety features and technique that the car had. I so wished to have that car, but after inquiring about the price, I took a step back. Not only was the car costly, but it was only available in New Delhi, and couldn't be delivered interstate. As disappointed as I was, that car didn't leave my mind. After almost a year, I came to know that a new Volvo showroom had been inaugurated in Jaipur, and the company had launched a new model whose price was lower than the one I had driven but still had all the features that I had loved. It was like my dream had come true when I came to know. Immediately. I booked my car and my wish was fulfilled.

When we think positive, we become positive and only grow better, keeping our mind healthy.

So can we consciously influence our subconscious mind? Can we choose to give it only positive thoughts?

We can never have a complete control over our subconscious mind, but there are ways in which we can influence it and make it active:

1. **Meditation:** Our mind is continuously filled with thoughts. Our mind is super active throughout the day. So first of all, calm your mind. Get in contact with your subconscious mind. It will help you channelise your thoughts.

2. **Visualisation:** Build a picture of what you want. Imagine yourself in a role or achieving a result you wished. For this, you can also create an album and can go through it from time to time.

3. **Writing thoughts:** you can also write down your wishes and feelings on paper so that it can declutter your thoughts and feelings and better understand your subconscious mind and yourself.

4. **Positive affirmations:** Repeating positive thoughts and mantras can help us focus and communicate with our minds. Self-affirmation helps maintain a positive self-view.

5. **Intuition:** The little voice in your head is your intuition. Learn to listen to it to figure out what it's trying to tell you. You can improve your intuitive abilities in several ways, such as by paying attention to sudden insights or practising mindfulness.

I am worthy of love

I am worthy of rest

I am worthy of kindness

I am worthy of respect

I am worthy of joy

I am worthy of compassion

> *Affirm. Affirm all things positive everyday. Lift yourself up and be the version of yourself.*

Our thoughts give birth to our dreams and wishes, and our strong beliefs help us achieve them. The majority of us tend to take our minds for granted despite the immense power it holds. When our ideas continuously run through our minds for the entire day, we assume that we do not have control over what we think. But the reality is, it's us who decides what we think about, and what we think about is what we become. As soon as we realise and accept it, it is our mind's true hidden power. It's not really a secret. Everyone, including you, has access to this power for free.

You are exactly what you think about, and this is "the secret." By thinking positive things, you can bring about the changes you desire in your life. You end up being exactly who you think you are.

How to use your mind's power?
Start thinking about your life and where you want to be. Picture it in your mind, and keep thinking about it throughout the day. Believe in it. Be self-assured that you are capable of turning this perfect picture into reality.

Now you will see that your actions automatically start aligning in accordance with what you see. You are going to move in the correct direction by taking baby steps.

When you choose what you want,
you automatically align with it
and it becomes your reality.

You'll also have obstacles, but you need to make it a point to not let them deter you. If you keep a clear image of the life you want to build in your mind at all times, you will eventually translate that life into your reality.

You have to start right now. And you will achieve all that you wanted in your life. Have faith in yourself. It is only our strong belief that can help us in becoming what we want. We all know this, "thing good, achieve good".

We need to always think positively but often, we are unable to follow these rules. When we are unhappy in life where we are, we try to change and turn to different escapes. We party or buy materialistic things to boost our happiness. So we try to change our environment in the hope that everything will change. But unfortunately, that's not how changes work. Why? because we erroneously believe that this external change is the beginning of a better life. It is true that our environment has an effect on our circumstances, but this approach doesn't address the underlying problem - your thought process - which motivates your feelings.

If you want to be what you think. Then firstly, bring the change from inside instead of outside. You need to change the way you think because what you think directly affects how you feel. How you feel directly affects how your body reacts.

What we think, translates into our actions and makes it our reality.

How your body reacts directly affects how you act, and how you act directly affects who you are and what you experience in life.

Thoughts don't have a power of their own. Only when we pay attention to them, do they start to seem real. When we start putting fuel on them by thinking about them more, we begin to feel the emotions that stem from those thoughts. This changes our emotional state, which then changes how we act.

If you think, "yes, I can do it." You regularly engage with the thought that you are successful and pay more attention to it. You will be more confident with a positive state of mind. Your body will act similarly. Your body language will be more confident, you'd be standing straight, energised, and happy, but on the other hand, if you engage with negative thoughts, you will feel discouraged and perhaps depressed. How will your body react to this? You will sulk down, slump your shoulders, and there will be no confidence.

Thoughts trigger emotions. How you think and feel directly impacts how your body reacts, and all three impact your behaviour and actions. This results in your emotional state being: agitated, depressed, discouraged, pleased, invigorated, happy, confident, and so forth. This is how your thoughts manifest into your world. You define who you are and what you experience in life by how you behave and act.

> *Our thoughts are the investments we make to form our future. This is a fixed deposit that contributes to our prosperity in the longer run.*

So whatever we are experiencing in our life is due to our thoughts. Start thinking positively, and build a strong belief. We are capable of achieving our goals. We are the ones who are making our world within our own heads. It will depend on whether or not we want to cultivate a rose garden or flowers that are toxic to humans. A person who is very determined and who makes alterations to the way he thinks has the ability to rule the entire globe. When you have made up your mind to climb Mt. Everest, there is nothing that can stop you from doing it.

> *Think positive, Live happily,*
> *Make your life extraordinary.*

Let's List Down The Factors That You Want To Be Truly A Part Of Your Life. Let's Think About The Factors That You Think Will Add To Making Your Life Extraordinary

1. **Visualisation:** Create A Visual Board For Yourself And Put Images Of The Things You Want In Your Life, Like: Your Dream Car, Your Dream Home, And Your Most Desired Paycheck And Place This Collage In A Place Where You Can See It On A Daily Basis.

2. **Journaling:** Start Maintaining A Thought Journal And Keep It With You All The Time. Anytime, Anywhere Anything That May Resonate With You, Pen It Down. The Moment You Start Doing That, You Will Start Aligning With Your Ultimate Goals And Dreams.

3. **Affirm:** Think About Positives, Count Your Strengths, And List Them Down. Keep Adding To Your List Of Strengths So That It Keeps Growing. Every Time You List A New One, Go Through All The Ones You Have Listed Before.

Chapter 8

THINK BIG, BECOME SUCCESSFUL

> *"Keep your cherished photos of your destiny at the fore front of your mind. No one gets the gut to make them blurred. Always think about it; dream about it and work it out!"*
>
> **~Tim Ferriss**

In the last chapter, we understood how important our thought process is. Whatever we get in life is the outcome of our thoughts. When we want to live happily, we take action accordingly. Now let me tell you about another way through which you can make your life happy. It holds true in all areas of our life - social, financial, family, and physical fields.

Each one of us wants to be happy and successful in life. But still, only a few of them are able to make it. Then what is it that we need to do? Think big. Why do we want to limit our thoughts by aiming small when life in itself is long and big? To succeed, we have to think and aim much higher than what we are thinking.

We should set goals that are much bigger than what we think we can do, and we should take massive actions much bigger than what we think we need to do to reach those goals.

The biggest mistake most people make is setting limited goals and hence limiting their actions. Why have we limited ourselves to smaller things when God has created such a big planet? God has given us a brain to think and lots of potential to take action to make our thoughts into reality. We shouldn't limit ourselves to small happiness. There is a lot that is yet to come into your life.

The majority of people are unable to think to the extent successful people think. If you haven't reached the top, you should question what you are doing and thinking. If you limit your potential, you will also limit your success. Be ready to go above and beyond, even if other people think it's crazy.

Usually, we set goals that aren't high enough. We think that if we have a lot of small things, we can build something big. We have many huge possibilities, but we don't believe in ourselves and think we can't do it. Some of the things we do just waste our time, energy, and money.

When our targets or work is not done within our limit, and we need to know how much effort is required, we get discouraged and disappointed. We should assume that our work will require ten times more effort, time, and money than what we think. If it doesn't happen, that's great, but you'll be mentally ready if it does.

what you think
you deserve

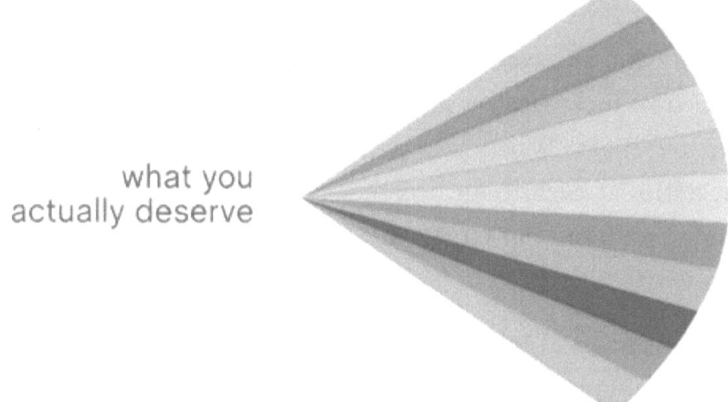

what you
actually deserve

NEVER underestimate yourself. We refrain from aiming higher in such a state of mind. REALIZE YOUR VALUE.

If you go home, by the route which is always packed with heavy traffic jams and you reach home late daily, then you will be mentally prepared before leaving your office. When it takes more effort than what you expected to meet your set goals, many people shift to the finish line rather than fueling the necessary actions. Successful people push people to do more, even if they must meet the goal. They don't limit the goal. No matter how high our goal is, there will always be problems because life constantly changes.

When it's hard to get small things done, it's better to set bigger goals from the beginning. It is our job and duty to live happily and successfully. It is said that successful people make their own luck because success leads to more success. It works like a magnet. When you achieve your intended goal, being successful at everything becomes your habit. It then compels you to set more big targets and to continue to achieve bigger goals.

This habit of winning becomes your nature. Just thinking is not enough to become king, it is also important to back that approach with action. To become a king, you will need the required effort and time. You have to do massive action. When we see successful people like the Ambanis or Tatas, we praise their achievements, but we forget how much effort, sacrifice and time they have given to achieve that success.

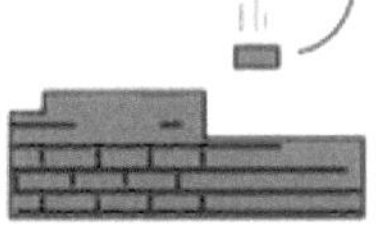

> *The greatness of our thought, amplifies our efforts. We must build bigger and stronger walls to create fortresses.*

Rome was not built in a day. Success is not something you get overnight.

> *"Success is not something that happens to you; it is something that happens because of you and because of the actions that you take."*

Success or failure are the two sides of a coin. When we achieve our goals we feel very happy. Our confidence boosts up, and we think we have a sense of achievement. But when we fail, we start blaming others for not getting the work done. When we accept the accountability of success, we should also do the same for failure. Instead of making excuses for failure, we should make more effort to achieve our targets. There can not be only one way to success. If one door closes, we should try for another one which can help us to get to our target.

Aimless people make excuses. They do not want to do anything. Excuses are the reasons why you don't have to do anything. Making excuses for your faults or failures is just a way to cover them up. People who are uncomfortable with the idea of taking on duties and responsibilities are likely to find unjustified excuses to get out of doing anything productive. Whereas, people who are successful never make excuses. Instead, they look for solutions to every difficulty. To become successful, we have to think bigger, because average thinking can keep us limited.

If you want to increase your sales by 10% and you have targeted to increase them by 20% only and you may be able to only achieve 5% of the target. You will not be able to achieve what you wanted but if you set the target for 50% and you are able to achieve 5% of that, you'd still be in profit.

Any project where you settle for average will not be successful and you will end up not achieving your goals sooner or later. Nothing in life works with an average approach. If you don't pay much attention to something, it will start to deter and eventually diminish. An average approach never gives more than average results. In fact, most of the time it gives even less than what you'd want. If you think and act like everyone else, you will only be miserable, uncertain, and fail. Get rid of everything average in your life. You have to compromise for everything in an average state of mind. So, set your goals bigger. You are doing this for yourself, not for others.

When you make bigger goals, sometimes you are afraid of whether you will be able to achieve them or not and you take a step back. Instead, you should use it as fuel. When you feel scared, you must face your fear and do something immediately.

When we reach our goals, some people will be happy for us, but most may be unhappy. As a result, they would be critical of your journey.

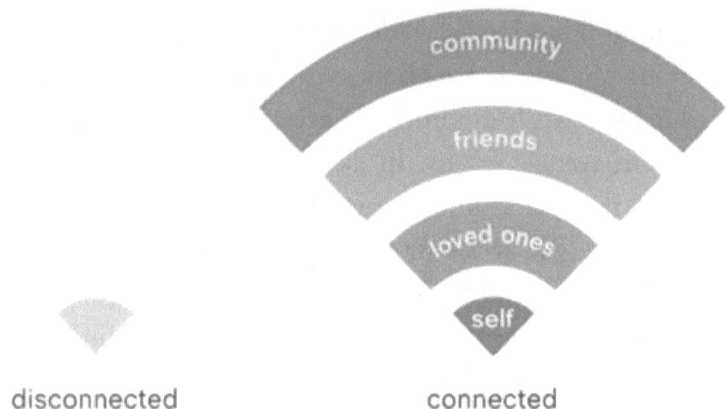

Let's connect! Connect with each other/ build communities and achieve greater heights to build an extraordinary life!

We don't like being criticised. But such criticism shows that you've done well. When you get criticised, you are on the right path and you are doing the right thing. As soon as you do something big, people will start telling you their opinions and what they think about it. They will be more aware of everything you do. But you shouldn't be afraid of what other people think because they are the kind of people who don't try very hard to improve their lives. We should not get affected by such criticism. If we let it affect us then, we can never use our full potential. Such critics stop when they realise that anything that they have to say doesn't affect us and we continue to rise. Sooner than later, their criticism will turn into appreciation.

Successful people talk differently, think differently, and handle situations, difficulties, and issues differently than most people. Successful people have certain set habits, routines, and skills that make them successful. We can also be successful by doing what they do and thinking the way they do.

Following are a few tips that can help you achieve success:

- You will be successful if you look at every situation with a solution-oriented mindset and a can-do attitude.

- Say "yes" to opportunities, accept challenges, and find solutions to problems.

- Keep yourself going, don't give up, and keep at it until you succeed.

- Be brave and take risks that are hard, unreasonable, and dangerous.

- Make money by trading new ideas, products, services, and ways to solve problems.

- Focus on what you want to achieve and what you are doing right now.

- Learn new things all the time, be open to change, and think outside the box.

- Make your own reality and decide which way to go.

- Respect the people in your company or who are more successful than you.

Think About All The Aspirations You Have. Think About How Successful You Want To Be. Now, It's Time For You To Expand Your Thoughts And Magnify Your Aspirations.

In The Table Below, List Down Your Present Aspirations And Then Multiply Their Magnitude By 10.

Ambitions You Had Set For Yourself	Your New Set of Higher Ambitions

Now That You Have A List of Your Bigger Ambitions, Align Them With The Necessary Actions You Need To Take For You To Achieve Them.

Your New Set of Higher Ambitions	Your New Set of Higher Efforts

Chapter 9

THINGS TO KEEP IN MIND

There are many other things in life from which we can learn and grow. The main subject points have been covered but there are more factors that need to be considered in our life. Throughout the entire journey of this book, we have learned, conquered, and driven through a rollercoaster of emotions, aspects, and sides of our life. Let's together go through and assess what are other areas where we can further incorporate work to make our extraordinary life.

1. Discipline

Discipline is a set of rules, management, and order that helps keep life going in a natural flow. It helps keep things balanced. It helps us to figure out our actions and the way to do them. Discipline is a big reason why most adults are successful. Maintaining a good performance at work, and taking care of your health as you get older are the important areas that require some discipline. Social discipline means acting in a civil manner at meetings, events, or gatherings. Professional discipline is mostly about managing time, meeting deadlines, greeting seniors properly, keeping healthy relationships, and so on. Unlike "terms and conditions," which are made to fit their own needs, discipline should always be made to fit the needs of the individual first. But it is necessary to be mindful of not overdoing it. It restricts our mental boundaries. Because of this, either our relationships break or we miss out on opportunities.

We tend to become judgemental or biassed, towards people who don't follow our biases and hence our productivity reduces. We start judging and being harsh on others and ourselves. Be flexible to some extent in circumstances so that you can breathe and let others breathe too.

> *Align, discipline, be organized and conquer life!*

2. Learn To Listen

Sometimes we speak so much that we don't listen to others. This results in missing out on generous advice, which could be helpful for us. We consider ourselves to be so intelligent that we are not ready to consider the advice of others. So, we end up being impatient and lose the opportunity to gain another perspective. We should have an open ear to listen to what someone has to say in a conversation and be considerate enough to their point of view. Or to be responsive with small words or phrases for what the other person has to say. The other person will feel heard and respected. However, one must be careful not to interrupt the speaker in the middle of their thought. It can be interpreted as interference or as negligent behaviour. When someone doesn't feel heard, it feels bad and they end up making assumptions about you through this behaviour. It's important for our close friends and family to know that we care about them, and what better way than to listen to them when they need it? When we listen to other people, we need to be patient and vigilant. It's our responsibility to deal with them in a mature way and to be empathetic to them. Most problems happen because people don't know how to talk to each other. When we listen to other people, half of the problems get solved.

We don't listen to what other people have to say or care about, so we end up fighting and disagreeing with our coworkers. When things don't go our way, we get angry, impatient, overwhelmed, and whatnot. Instead of handling the situation wisely, we make bad choices that make things worse. When we listen to someone, we feel important and valued since someone reached out to us out of respect and trust. Often, we help them solve some problems. When we are good listeners, people often come to us just to talk about their problems. This is because people feel comfortable when they share their thoughts with others.

When we listen to someone instead of talking, we have time to think about what is going on and how it should be handled. When we listen to and judge people, we see all the pros and cons of the situation and make a decision based on that. This keeps us from making hasty choices, which we might have done if we hadn't thought things through. To figure things out, it's often important to listen to what people have to say instead of making up our own ideas. This is why we have meetings so that everyone's opinion can be heard and a decision can be made after taking into account all the reasonable opinions. When we listen to others, new ideas are generated that give birth to new inventions, and new opportunities.

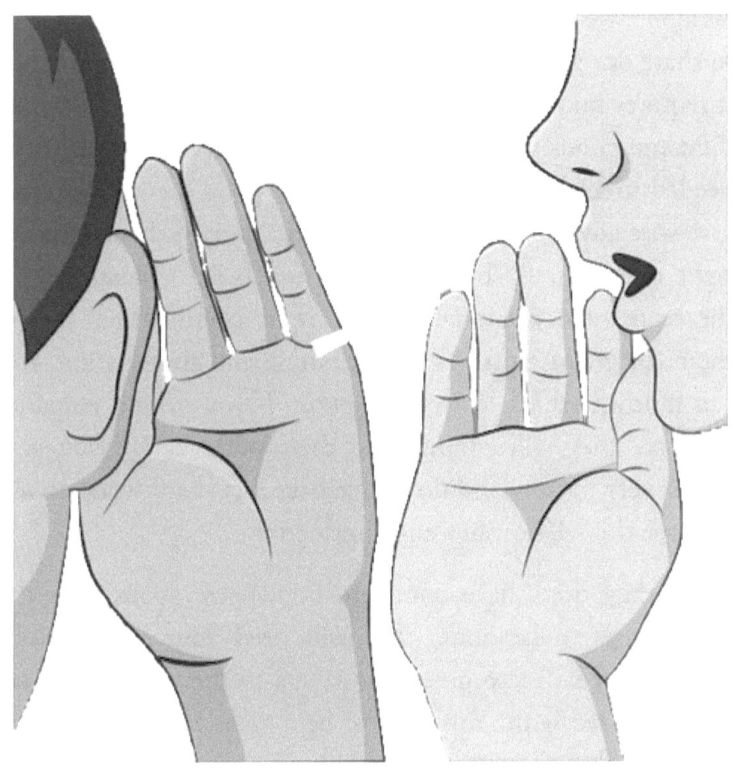

Don't just hear, LISTEN. A true listener
is what this world really needs.

3. Be A Mentor, Not A Dictator

Every human being is different from each other and so is the way we work. As stated earlier we can not live in this world all alone, we need people to celebrate, to get work done, and to share our feelings. Ideas can take birth from one mind, but it requires multiple hands for their execution. Then, how can different minds work on a single tangent? A good mentor is needed to lead a team. By becoming a good mentor, you can give wise advice to your team, you can provide them with the right resources. By building trust and belief systems within the team, you can establish the right coordination among them. By giving equal respect, freedom, and appreciation, you can motivate them to work together. If you exhibit empathy and care they will willingly do their work. But if you give orders very harshly and do not respect their hard work, it will hamper the relationship and productivity.

If they don't have complete knowledge about how the work needs to be done, they will need your guidance. In return, they will also give their 100% to the work they have been assigned with. You have to be a great listener and team leader so that they can share their ideas, and problems and can give solutions. For being successful, it is imperative to build a good team and lead it well.

BOSS

LEADER

TAKES CREDIT

GIVES CREDIT

Be a true leader, and take your people with you on this journey. Be a leader, not a dictator.

4. Respect Your Body

Your body is the system that makes everything happen for you in this world. No matter how much bigger you think, or what your aims are. If you don't take care of the home your soul resides in, it will not respect you in return. It is our duty to take care of our body, mind, and soul to gain the maximum input from it as it is capable of giving. Our body is a machine, it needs continuous maintenance. Along with the physical structure, our mind and soul are an integral part of our physicality. When we respect it, take care of it, be mindful of what goes in it, and make sure to exercise, take care of our mental health and be spiritually aligned, it will reflect in our work, interactions, and the world we make for ourselves.

5. Spirituality

Our lives are packed with action, movement, and daily hustle. It is a good practice to spare some of our time for aligning with our spirituality. Whether it is god, Allah, Bhagwan or one divine source of energy that you believe in, take some time to align your mind and heart with the superpower and to express your gratitude. We are blessed with so many things, so many facets and so many relationships. It is our moral duty to have some time for our spirituality. It will give you a sense of calmness, peace, and self-motivation. When we are calm, we are able to focus more on work. When you direct your energy to align with your spirituality, your zeal multiplies and your soul is re-energized with the power and faith of conquering the world.

> *Everything starts from you. It is your duty to treat your body like a temple and take care of your body, mind and soul.*

6. Pause And Recap Your Life

It is good to be motivated, but if not followed through with consistency, it is in vain. We tend to continue to hustle without taking a moment to pause and review, think, evaluate, correct, and move ahead stronger. Pauses are as important as sprints. Running towards your goals, all guns blazing is important, but it is also important to take small pauses to re-evaluate your course of action, make necessary amendments and then tread ahead even stronger. One bad day doesn't mean you have a bad life, don't lose hope or morale because of a few setbacks. Don't let the noise of ego overpower the calm of your confidence. Never lose sight of your one true purpose, only that, will be your true guiding hand and will lead you to true liberation and your highest self.

> *Life is teamwork. Everything we build or intend to build, can only be realized together with people, professionally or personally. Pause, evaluate and build.*

Chapter 10

CONCLUSION:
THIS IS YOUR EXTRAORDINARY LIFE

Life is a precious and valuable gift and opportunity given to us by the divine and it is our duty to make the most of it. We must pursue our vision and purpose and make the journey of life meaningful, full of growth, new experiences, and positive contributions to the world. It is crucial to step out of our comfort zones, be open to change, and strive for happiness and satisfaction. Expressing gratitude and appreciating the good in our lives is vital to lead a fulfilling and joyful life. By recognizing and being thankful for what we have, we gain a clearer understanding of our lives and stay grounded. Focusing on the present moment and dedicating time to our passions can bring peace and happiness into our lives. It is important to prioritise our well-being and take action towards creating the life we desire, rather than constantly putting it off.

Making big decisions in life can be difficult, but change is a crucial aspect of growth. To grow continuously, we need to have an open mind towards diversity and change and be willing to adapt. Change, whether in our surroundings or within ourselves, is necessary for growth. Fear is a common barrier that prevents us from realising our dreams and achieving success. However, it is important to remember that even successful people have fears, but they choose to focus on their goals and not let fear control their lives.

sometimes when you feel stuck

you're actually growing in a different way

that is preparing you for an extraordinary new chapter in your life

> ***Everything that happens in our lives is a divine orchestration. Even when things are not going as per what you think, you're growing to be prepared for something which is bigger than what you could ever imagine.***

By identifying our values, mindset, and priorities, we can create a plan to reach our destination. This requires taking responsibility for our choices and being truthful with ourselves. With the help of the seven components of the wheel of life, we can work on improving areas that need attention and strive for a balanced and fulfilling life.

Relationships are the basis of a happy and successful life. They provide the physical, mental and emotional support we need to overcome challenges and reach our goals. Our loved ones, who are there to support us and push us forward, are our biggest resources. With the right team in place, we can conquer the world and make our dreams a reality.

The power of our subconscious mind is the magic behind our achievements if we influence it positively and can help us achieve our desires. By practising techniques like meditation, visualisation, writing thoughts, positive affirmations, and intuition, we can tap into the power of our subconscious mind to make our dreams a reality. Remember, everything starts with our thoughts, and our subconscious mind acts on them, so choose your thoughts wisely.

Discipline is important to balance and order our life, but we need to be mindful not to overdo it. Good listening skills are crucial in relationships, problem-solving and generating new ideas. Finally, being a mentor helps in building trust, coordination and motivation within a team. To lead effectively, we need to listen, provide guidance and show empathy and respect. By incorporating these values into our lives, we can continue to grow and achieve success in our personal and professional lives.

Let us embrace change, overcome our fears, and unlock the full potential of life. By accepting ourselves for who we are, we can close the gap between our current selves and our desired selves, and lead an extraordinary life that is truly ours. It's time to embrace the power of relationships and start building your dream team today. But, the key is you. The key is to have a strong belief and positive thoughts to achieve what you think.

Just like me, you too can choose to take the first step, overcome your fears, and convert them into your strength, making the impossible possible. So, let's not be afraid to take that leap of faith, and live our lives to the fullest.

You are the master of your own life and should not let your circumstances dictate your decisions. Let us be brave enough to make conscious choices and move ahead with a passion to live life to the fullest. Let's all of us come together, to not only make our lives better but also those who are spread throughout this whole world. Let's join hands and build a strong community.

Follow us on.................................and look out for workshops, to experience the magic and the aura of positivity.

Let's build together and succeed together! Let's make each life extraordinary.

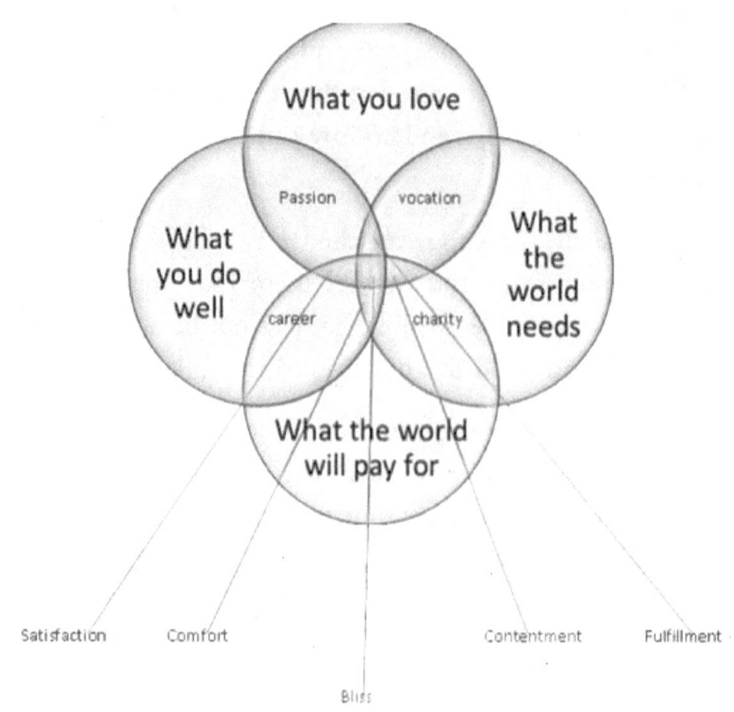

> ## THIS.
> ### *This is an extraordinary life.*
> ### *This is YOUR EXTRAORDINARY LIFE!*